royal
london

OTHER TITLES
IN THIS SERIES

Bloody London

royal
london

The haunts and hideouts of kings
and queens from London's
past and present

Karen Pierce-Goulding

crimson

Royal London: The haunts and hideouts of kings and queens from London's past and present
This first edition published in 2012 by
Crimson Publishing Ltd
Westminster House
Kew Road
Richmond
Surrey
TW9 2ND

© Crimson Publishing 2012

Author Karen Pierce-Goulding

British Library Cataloguing in Publication Data
A catalogue record for this book is available from the British
Library

ISBN 978 1 78059 070 7

Typeset by RefineCatch Ltd, Bungay, Suffolk
Printed and bound in the UK by Ashford Colour Press, Gosport, Hants

To Mary & David Tucker of London Walks (www.walks.com) with love and thanks.

... and to my daughter Isobella, who shares her Daddy's boundless energy and enthusiasm for learning new things.

CONTENTS

ABOUT THE AUTHOR

Karen Pierce-Goulding is a winner of the prestigious Blue Badge Guide of the Year award and was listed by *Travel + Leisure* magazine as one of their World's Greatest Tour Guides. A journalist and reformed actress, Karen loves to tell a good story and she and her husband, Adam, both regularly 'shout their heads off in the street' leading walking tours for London Walks. Karen lives in North London.

INTRODUCTION

At times, the Royal Family can seem distant from everyday London life. They are the stuff of period drama or titillating tabloid tales. All very entertaining but actually irrelevant to modern London living.

Yet an ordinary London day is touched in dozens of subtle ways by the extraordinary tales of royal history.

If you've ever changed trains at Victoria, walked along Kingsway or shopped on Regent Street, you are brushing up against the Royal Family.

If you've ever had a drink at the King's Head, or taken up a sunny spot in Kensington Gardens, or if you've ever hired a dinner jacket, then, once again, the Royal Family are very near at hand.

Study at King's College? A night at the theatre in Haymarket or Drury Lane? Or the famous Proms? Too highbrow? Well how about a return to the pub and a night in the White Hart at Mile End. If you think this last course of action will take you away from the Royal Family, then think again.

And we haven't even mentioned palaces yet. We've plenty of those.

This book attempts to bring to life some of those more arcane London locations shaped by royal history – as well as detailing the famous landmarks of Royal London. As we chase the ghosts of King Henry VIII and Queen Elizabeth I, we'll meet the current Royal Family and follow their footsteps through the modern-day metropolis.

I hope you enjoy our trip along the Queen's highway(s)... and byways.

KPG
London, April 2012

1 ROYAL KENSINGTON

Kensington has royal connections that go back to the Conqueror, when King William I granted land to one Geoffrey de Mowbray – who, in turn, gave tenancy to Aubrey de Vere. The de Veres later became the Earls of Oxford – hence the name of nearby Earls Court.

Great shopping, high-end dining, rich in history, rich in culture, sometimes just plain rich, there's even a bona fide royal palace. The phrase 'very Kensington' becomes a byword for regality and luxury.

Kensington Palace (1)

Kensington Gardens, W8 4PX. See www.hrp.org.uk/KensingtonPalace for prices and opening times. Tube: Queensway

Kensington Palace is one of those London buildings that divides opinion: some are of a mind that it is somewhat plain to behold; others think that it's downright bleak and looks more like an orphanage than a palace.

But when we throw the two magic words 'Christopher Wren' in the direction of its red brick façade, a little architectural fairy dust sticks to the old place. Its clean, classical lines suddenly become more elegant. Its dark windows suddenly seem less foreboding and more like a welcome.

The Duke of Windsor (formerly Prince of Wales, briefly King Edward VIII) once commented on the number of royals living at Kensington Palace by waggishly dubbing it 'an aunt heap'.

The cast list of residents is an impressive one indeed.

DIANA, PRINCESS OF WALES

The newlywed Prince and Princess of Wales moved into apartments 8 and 9 in 1981. Diana lived here until her death in 1997. Her coffin rested here on 5 September 1997 before her final journey to Westminster Abbey and thence to Althorp. Princes William and Harry were raised here and Prince William made a return of sorts in 2011 when it was announced that he and the Duchess of Cambridge would use Kensington Palace as their official London residence.

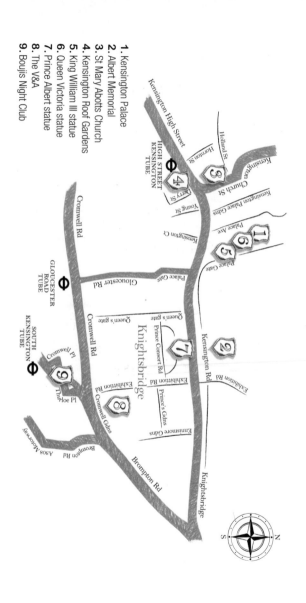

1. Kensington Palace
2. Albert Memorial
3. St Mary Abotts Church
4. Kensington Roof Gardens
5. King William III statue
6. Queen Victoria statue
7. Prince Albert statue
8. The V&A
9. Boujis Night Club

QUEEN VICTORIA

In 1819, Prince Edward, Duke of Kent and Strathearn and Earl of Dublin (fourth son of George III) and Princess Victoria of Saxe-Coburg-Saalfeld had a daughter, born here at the palace, who would go on to reign over us (happy and glorious) for longer than anyone else… so far.*

PRINCESS MARGARET

Princess Margaret, late sister of HM Queen Elizabeth II, lived at Kensington Palace. These past few years have been open season for documentary-makers keen to present the more lurid aspects of the Princess's life on screen. Suffice it to say, all have been broadcast after the 9pm watershed. How many of the details can be proven as fact is not my job to say. But one detail did amuse…

The Princess was famed for enjoying her food and would tuck in with great alacrity… thus posing a problem for her royal guests. Royal etiquette dictates that, when dining with the Royal Family, should the hosts put down the eating irons, then you, the guest, must stop eating too. If one wanted to enjoy the fruits of the wonderful kitchens at Kensington, one therefore had to attack the meal with gusto, before the plates were taken away.

KING WILLIAM III

First monarch to live here – from 1689; first monarch to die here – in 1702. Preferred the fresh air of countrified Kensington (!) to the damp of the riverbank Palace of Whitehall.

PRINCE AND PRINCESS MICHAEL OF KENT

HM The Queen's cousins became the subject of a minor royal controversy – or, if you prefer, a royal minor controversy – when their Kensington Palace rent for apartment 10 was raised to a more – ahem – competitive level. The new rent was set at £120,000 per year, a leap of around £116,000 from the nominal rent paid hitherto.

(*At the time of writing, Her Maj E2 is rubbing along quite nicely, thanks for asking. In May 2011 she became the second-longest-reigning monarch, nudging George III into bronze medal position. Queen Victoria's long-standing royal record hangs in the balance and is due to be toppled in September 2015.)

PETER THE WILD BOY

At first he may sound like an inappropriate chum of Prince Harry, but Peter the Wild Boy was actually a foundling teenager who lived at the court of King George I in 1726 and 1727. Found naked and mute in the woods outside Hanover in Germany, Peter lived to the ripe old age of 70, by which time he is reported to have a clear understanding of speech, but a practical vocabulary of only three words: 'Peter' and 'King George'.

The Albert Memorial (2)

Kensington Gardens. Tube: South Kensington/Gloucester Road

You could live in London for half a lifetime before you ever ran into a Londoner who says: 'The Albert Memorial? I don't have an opinion either way.'

Everyone has an opinion on the Albert Memorial.

Delete as applicable: 'Sir George Gilbert Scott's Albert Memorial is the apex of Victorian ingenuity and creativity and symbolises vividly the reach-for-Heaven-and-beyond ethos of Victorian ambition.' Or: 'Sir George Gilbert Scott's Albert Memorial stands as testament to the excess and vanity of an empire that not only subjugated its colonists but enslaved its own citizens right here in the East End of London.'

Answers on a postcard, please.

In the meantime, here come the statistics: 176 feet tall, 20 years in the making, cost £120,000. Restored in 1994 at a cost of £10 million – roughly the modern equivalent of the original cost.

Sir George Gilbert Scott is responsible for the memorial, while the golden figure of Albert is the work of John Foley.

St Mary Abbots Church (3)

Kensington Church Street, W8 4LA. Tube: High Street Kensington

The present church dates from 1872 and was designed by that man again, Sir George Gilbert Scott (see also the Albert Memorial).

The church has a pew reserved for royal parishioners in the front row, which dates back to Queen Victoria's reign. It also boasts a memorial to Alfred, Duke of Edinburgh and of Saxe-Coburg and Gotha (d.1900), and Leopold, Duke of Albany (d.1884), sons of Queen Victoria, sculpted by their sister Princess Louise.

In the autumn of 1997, the church became a focal point for mourners after the death of Diana, Princess of Wales.

Kensington Roof Gardens (4)

99 Kensington High Street, W8 5SA. Access is via Derry Street, just off Kensington High Street. Tube: High Street Kensington

Kensington Roof Gardens can be found atop the old Derry & Toms department store, which was bought in 1920 by neighbouring department store John Barker. Currently owned by Sir Richard Branson, the gardens are open to the general public most days, free of charge. They can be booked out for launch parties and private functions and at such times they are closed to the public.

Barker kept Derry & Toms trading as a shop for respectable middle-class goods, keeping the John Barker department store at the high end of the market, angling for a more Harrods-like clientele. Swinging Sixties outfitter Biba moved into the old Derry & Toms building in 1974 but closed soon after. In the 1960s, Princess Anne, like many a teenage girl, shopped at Biba. The Roof Gardens were the venue for a party in July 2011 at which the Duchess of Cambridge was pictured dancing with chum-in-chief to the young royal set, nightclub owner Guy Pelly.

THREE KENSINGTON STATUES

Kingly statue: King William III (5)
A jaunty fellow, by the looks of this tribute by Heinrich Baucke; King Billy's statue was donated to the nation in 1907 by Kaiser Wilhelm II to his Uncle Ted (King Edward VII) – perhaps in an effort to highlight the blood ties between the two nations in a sticky diplomatic period to dispel the clouds of war. It failed.

Queenly statue: Queen Victoria (6)
Of all the statues of Queen Victoria in London, this is the one that tends to surprise most people. The very words 'Queen Victoria' conjure up but one image: a more mature lady; dressed in black; not necessarily laughing (not amused, etc., etc.) This statue, however, was made from a series of likenesses taken when HM was but 19 years old, the age at which she became Queen. It is the work of her daughter (working retrospectively) Princess Louise, a talented sculptress. Louise caused something of a scandal in her day by marrying a commoner. He was the Duke of Argyll, but then everyone is a commoner when your ma is Queen of England and Empress of India.

> **Consort statue: Prince Albert (7)**
> He's got a memorial. He's got a great big hall. Which is perhaps why we let this 'modest' bronze slip our minds, tucked as it is behind the Royal Albert Hall. It's the work of Joseph Durham and dates from 1858, predating its big brother, the Gothic skyrocket that is the Albert Memorial, by some 14 years.

Elsewhere in the borough...

The Royal Borough of Kensington & Chelsea was created in 1965, when the boroughs of Kensington and Chelsea were yoked together. Kensington has enjoyed Royal Borough status since 1901, in accordance with the wishes of the late Queen Victoria who was born here (see page 5). It has long been the playground of royals...

KING'S ROAD

Tube: Sloane Square

Since 1955, when Mary Quant opened Bazaar at no. 138a – widely held to be Britain's first boutique shop – King's Road has been a shopping Mecca for the bright young things of London.

Catherine (back when she was just plain ol' Kate Middleton) was spotted doing a little pre-wedding shopping here. According to the *Daily Telegraph* she even purchased a 'Kate blouse' – a garment identical to the one she wore for her famous engagement portrait by Mario Testino – from Whistles. The *Telegraph* also spotted 2011's most famous bride-to-be popping into Banana Republic while *Metro* and the *Daily Mirror* followed her into Warehouse. In the aftermath of the wedding, Chelsy Davy, ex-girlfriend of Prince Harry, was pictured in the *Daily Mail* buying a pair of black patent wedge shoes similar in style to those sported by the new Duchess of Cambridge.

The road takes its name from King Charles II, who travelled to Kew via a private road that existed here until the early 19th Century.

WORLD'S END

Tube: Sloane Square/West Brompton

An area at the western end of the King's Road, named after a tavern that was known to King Charles II. World's End is also the name of a King's Road shop owned by Vivienne Westwood and located at no. 430. In a previous incarnation, the shop was known as SEX and was frequented by the disaffected youth of the Bromley Contingent, including the embryonic Sex Pistols – who would go on to attempt to upstage Her Majesty in her Silver Jubilee year of 1977.

EXHIBITION ROAD

Tube: South Kensington

Exhibition Road is home to three major museums – Science, Natural History and V&A – founded in the aftermath of the Great Exhibition of 1851, in which Prince Albert was a major mover and shaker.

The nickname for the area favoured by current tourism chiefs is Museumland: which, at present, stubbornly refuses to catch the imagination of the general public. The old nickname for the area was Albertopolis – a title applied by both admirers and detractors of the Prince and his eagerness to be involved in the cultural advancement of the nation.

VICTORIA & ALBERT MUSEUM (8)

Cromwell Road, SW7 2RL. Open daily 10am–5.45pm, Fridays 10pm. Admission free. Tube: South Kensington

The world's largest museum of decorative arts and design is home to some 4.6 million objects. Queen Victoria laid the foundation stone for Sir Aston Webb's Cromwell Road entrance (he also designed Admiralty Arch in Westminster) in 1899, her last major public engagement, but it was not until 1909 that King Edward VII opened the structure. This façade is adorned with figures of Queen Victoria, Prince Albert, King Edward VII and Queen Alexandra.

BOUJIS NIGHTCLUB (9)

43 Thurloe Street, SW7 2LQ. Tube: South Kensington

Thurloe Street is named after a secretary of Oliver Cromwell: the perfect ironic spot in which to indulge in some seriously non-Cromwellian carousing.

By the year 2009, Boujis nightclub was a byword for royal shenanigans by night – even though young royals had patronised the club for some 18 months before word reached the gossip columns. A small, hyper-exclusive venue with a capacity of under 200 and membership by invitation only, in recent years the club has operated a policy whereby flash stars with large entourages are turned away. This is to avoid overcrowding the club with guests and having to turn away valued members.

The house cocktail and choice of royal revellers is the Crack Baby – even royal venues are not immune from the 1980s-born craze of distastefully named cocktails. As with all cocktails, variations are the stuff of heated debate, with some recipes involving fruit purée and electric blenders. But if the gossip columns are to be believed, the drink should be downed in one, which would make the following recipe the most practical:

1 Fl. oz vodka
1 Fl. oz champagne
1 Fl. oz passion fruit juice
one dash Chambord

To compound the bad taste of the name, if you've chosen to shake the cocktail with ice, the drink should be served in a test tube. Otherwise, bung the whole lot in a shot glass and repeat until you end up falling over and landing on the front page of the *Daily Mail* in March 2007 (see Prince Harry).

According to *Harper's Bazaar*, Tuesday is the night to be seen at Boujis. We've listed the nearest tube above, but we doubt that many of the members of this fabled London nightspot ever arrive in such a fashion.

HARRODS

87–135 Brompton Road, SW1X 7XL. Tube: Knightsbridge

A secondary focal point for mourners following the death of Diana, Princess of Wales. Dodi Fayed, son of Harrods' then-owner Mohamed Al-Fayed, was killed in the same car crash.

Prince Philip withdrew his royal warrant from Harrods in late 2000. Royal warrants are reviewed every five years and Prince Philip's visits to Harrods had declined sufficiently to remove the warrant.

Soon after, Mr Al-Fayed took the decision to remove the warrants of HM The Queen, HRH The Queen Mother and HRH The Prince of Wales, thus severing all royal trading relationships of his own volition.

At the end of the documentary film *Unlawful Killing* (at the time of writing, the film is yet to be given a UK screening for legal reasons), funded by Al-Fayed, the tycoon is filmed burning the royal warrants that once adorned the front of his store, in the grounds of his estate near his son's mausoleum. 'They were a curse,' said the Egyptian-born tycoon at the time, 'and business tripled following their removal.'

(Ali Al-Fayed, younger brother of the former Harrods owner, still trades under the royal warrant of the Prince of Wales as president and CEO of Turnbull & Asser, the Jermyn Street shirtmaker.)

Harrods had been entitled to bill themselves as being 'By Royal Appointment' since 1913, when they were awarded their first royal warrant. The store's motto is *Omnia Omnibus Ubique* – translated as 'All Things for All People, Everywhere'. Although, given the store's strict customer dress code, perhaps *Omnia Omnibus Ubique (Nisi Illud Populus Contingo Taedium Brevis)* – or 'All Things for All People, Everywhere (Unless Those People Are Wearing Shorts)' would be more appropriate.

In 2010, Mohamed Al-Fayed sold Harrods to the Qatar Investment Company.

Tired of shopping in Kensington? Try these royal alternatives...

HAWES & CURTIS

33–34 Jermyn Street, SW1Y 6HP. Tube: Piccadilly Circus

Shirtmaker to the man who would – briefly – be King Edward VIII. As Prince of Wales, Edward became something of a style and fashion leader. Preferring a bulky knot in his tie, he had his tailor cut his neckties wider than usual. With this bulky knot, a spread collar was required. Enter Hawes & Curtis of Jermyn Street (founded 1913) – who would also launder shirts for the Prince upon request. NB: It is erroneously believed that the Windsor Knot was named after the Prince, when in fact it was dubbed thus in honour of his equally stylish grandfather, King Edward VII. Which brings us to...

HENRY POOLE & CO.

15 Savile Row, W1S 3PJ. Tube: Oxford Circus

When, as Prince of Wales, King Edward VII approached Poole's (established in 1806) to tailor a comfortable, non-restrictive coat in which to dine and smoke, the great Savile Row tailor bent himself to the task with style and speed. The resulting shorter, single-button jacket with silk lapels delighted the Prince. At a Sandringham dinner party, one of his guests, an American chap by the name of James Potter, admired the jacket effusively. The Prince gave him Poole's details, and Mr Potter duly wore the jacket to his club, in Tuxedo Park NY. Thus the name tuxedo – the US term for dinner jacket – was born.

EDE & RAVENSCROFT

93 Chancery Lane, WC2A 1DU. Tube: High Holborn

This famous wig and gown-maker is obviously eager not to appear over-keen or vulgar – and so they simply state that their company is 'thought to be the oldest firm of tailors in the world'. At the time of writing, they hold a full set of royal warrants – enjoying the patronage of HM The Queen, HRH The Duke of Edinburgh and HRH The Prince of Wales. Ede & Ravenscroft first robed the royals for coronation when William and Mary became king and queen in 1689.

PARTRIDGE'S (UPMARKET GROCER)

2–5 Duke of York Square, SW3 4LY (off King's Road). Tube: Sloane Square

Established on the King's Road in 1972, Partridge's was awarded HM The Queen's royal warrant in 1994 – making it the Queen's grocer. Sources are divided as to what tea is favoured by Her Majesty, with some pointing to Darjeeling, others to Earl Grey. Partridge's are keeping their cards close to their chest with their Royal Blend loose tea (i.e. not in tea bags), describing it merely as a 'unique blend of Indian teas'. It retails at £3.50 for 125 grams.

   Catherine of Braganza, Queen Consort of King Charles II (after whom the shop's location, in King's Road, is named), introduced the custom of tea drinking to British society.

JOHN LOBB

9 St James's Street, SW1A 1EF. Tube: Piccadilly Circus

One can easily spot the King's Head and the King's Arms in London – those famous pub names can be seen swinging on signs all over town. But where can one see the King's legs? And the Queen's, come to that. In St James's, that's where. John Lobb have been bootmakers to the Royal Family since King Edward VII was Prince of Wales. As such they keep a last – the model around which a cobbler makes a shoe – fashioned to the exact shape of each customer's lower leg and foot.

CHARBONNEL ET WALKER

One The Royal Arcade, 28 Old Bond Street, W1S 4BT. Tube: Green Park

Chocolatier to HM The Queen, Mrs Walker and Mme Charbonnel opened for business in 1875 with the encouragement of – yes, him again – King Edward

VII when he was Prince of Wales. An early example, perhaps, of his enthusiasm for the *entente cordiale*. Given the Prince liked to dress well when dining well (see Henry Poole, page 11) and that he was fond of chocolate, it should perhaps come as no surprise that he also created the fashion for leaving the bottom button of the waistcoat (or vest in US parlance) undone – this simple expedient for allowing more comfort after the pudding course has become de rigueur among gentlemen everywhere.

HATCHARDS BOOKSHOP

187 Piccadilly, W1J 9LE. Tube: Piccadilly Circus/Green Park

The oldest bookshop in London – founded by John Hatchard in 1797 – Hatchards is currently in possession of a 'full house' of royal warrants: it is patronised by HM The Queen, HRH Prince Philip and HRH The Prince of Wales. High-profile writers are drawn to signings at Hatchards in greater number than to any other London bookshop. The Christmas Customer Evening, towards the end of November, can draw 20 or more big names from the world of literature, stationed throughout the store ready to sign your first editions.

Diana's Knightsbridge

COLEHERNE COURT

Old Brompton Road, SW5. Tube: Earls Court

From 1979 to 1981, no. 60 Coleherne Court was the home of Lady Diana Spencer. The three-bedroomed flat was an 18th birthday present from her parents. Those not-so-distant times are another country in terms of property prices: the cost of the property was in the region of £50,000. At the time of writing, during a downturn in the property market, a three-bedroom property in the same area was offered at £2,495,000, with another up for rent at £1,650 per week.

Diana moved from here to Clarence House in February 1981 on the eve of the announcement of her engagement – at that time, Clarence House was the residence of Queen Elizabeth, the Queen Mother.

A NICE SIT DOWN AND A CUP OF TEA

And is there honey still for tea?

As long as Kensington stands, the answer is a resounding yes.

On the main drag

The Orangery

Kensington Palace, W8 4PX. Tube: High Street Kensington/ Queensway

How to define Kensington? Well, one way could be to consider that when they take tea, Kensingtonites can do so in an 18th-century orangery designed by Christopher Wren. Toto, I don't think we're in Shepherd's Bush any more.

The Orangery is enormously popular and pot luck – perhaps teapot luck? – must be taken when heading here of an afternoon as they are unable to take bookings. It's worth the trip as, even if there's no table, the gardens are a joy to behold and the Royal Park – Kensington Gardens – provides ample space to sit and read and relax.

Something a little stronger, perhaps?

The Churchill Arms

119 Kensington Church Street, W8 7LN. Tube: Notting Hill Gate

There really is nowhere like The Churchill: Irish in flavour, named after Britain's great war hero and serving Thai food! It really shouldn't work but it jolly well does.

Sssshhh. It's a secret

The Scarsdale Tavern

23a Edwardes Square, W8 6HE. Tube: High Street Kensington/Kensington (Olympia)/Earl's Court

Well worth the yomp along to the western extremity of Kensington High Street, the Scarsdale exists in that 'other' Kensington: the hinterland of grandeur tucked away behind the shops and palaces and hullabaloo of central London.

2 ROYAL SOUTH LONDON

The wide open spaces of South London provide royal locations aplenty. Some of them are an easy walk from the 'centre-stage' Royal London of St James's or the West End (see Chapters 3 and 10). Others are entire neighbourhoods a little further off the beaten track for the regular London visitor and will require a train or bus ride – and, consequently, a little more time – to get there.

In stark contrast to North London (see Chapter 4), South London, in terms of royal locations, seems monarchist to the core. Perhaps this is one of the fundamental differences that result in the great north v. south debates here in the capital.

Where North London has royal fingerprints, its counterpart across the water boasts great tracts of land gouged out by royal hands and formed and moulded into battlefields, palaces and playgrounds. Indeed, the contrast is so great that one South London neighbourhood has a chapter all to itself: Greenwich (see Chapter 5).

In 2012 Greenwich became a Royal Borough. This new status was bestowed to celebrate HM's Diamond Jubilee. No such distinction can be found out to the north. In the pageant of royal history, all South London's a stage, to paraphrase a famous Midlander who got stuck down south, and with whose 'manor' we will begin our quest.

Bankside (1)

Tube/Rail: London Bridge

Far be it from me to cast aspersions on the morals of King Henry VIII, or indeed upon his chopping and changing, but this, ahem, colourful monarch had a great effect on the moral climate south of the river by attempting to outlaw prostitution.

Gentle reader, you might like to re-read that last sentence, going at odds as it does with everything you know about this romping monarch. (Our tabloids, had they been around, would have been in a permanent state of excitement at some of his antics.)

Yet that was exactly his course of action in the year 1546. Until this point, the landowners, who were the successive Bishops of Winchester, had tried only to

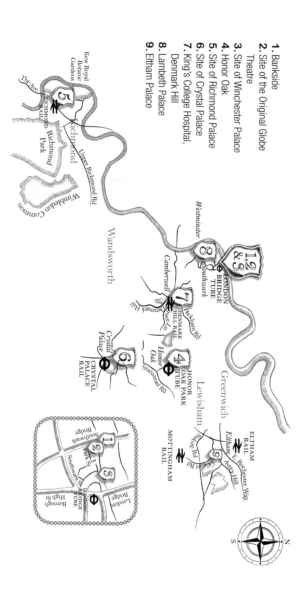

1. Bankside
2. Site of the Original Globe Theatre
3. Site of Winchester Palace
4. Honor Oak
5. Site of Richmond Palace
6. Site of Crystal Palace
7. King's College Hospital, Denmark Hill
8. Lambeth Palace
9. Eltham Palace

regulate the oldest profession. Given all we'd expect from religious leaders, you might like to read over *that* sentence again too.

The Original Globe Theatre and the Rose Theatre (2)

Rose Theatre: 56 Park Street, SE1 9AS. Tube: London Bridge

The original site of the Globe can be found in what is now Park Street. A plaque and a small exhibition mark the spot, upon which a Grade II listed Georgian terrace now stands.

Across the road a blue plaque issued by the people of the Borough of Southwark is positively tetchy in tone. It reads: 'The Rose Theatre Built Here in 1587'. So far, so deadpan. Beneath this statement of fact the wording continues: 'First Elizabethan theatre of Bankside'. Can I detect a tone of impatience at the spotlight-hogging Stratford Man and his 'wooden O'? Is this the plaque equivalent of the perennial understudy bemoaning his fate in the theatre bar after the show: 'That should have been me up there'?

Some of the original Globe's papers survive at Dulwich College in South London (founded by the actor Edward Alleyn, who was associated with the Rose from 1592). From these we know that Shakespeare's history play *King Henry IV Part 1* was staged here.

SHAKESPEARE'S HISTORY PLAYS

Shakespeare has long been a great springboard for debate, with some questioning the authorship of his plays and others entirely denying the existence of the Stratford Man. His History Plays (as grouped together in the First Folio of 1623 – the other two groupings being Tragedies and Comedies, the categories still broadly accepted today) have long been the subject of controversy among historians for their perpetuation of myth over fact, or for being Tudor propaganda pieces. One thing is certain: the plays have gone a long way in fuelling the popular images of those kings portrayed.

KING JOHN

No record exists of contemporary performance, and the earliest recorded production was at Drury Lane in 1737 (see Chapter 10).

RICHARD II

A specially commissioned performance of this play took place at the Globe on 7 February 1601. It was paid for by the supporters of the Earl of Essex and his rebellion against Queen Elizabeth I – the play's themes of usurpation being considered germane in the context.

HENRY IV PARTS 1 & 2 AND KING HENRY V

The usurper Bolingbroke is now king – and Act 1, Scene 1 is set at 'London: The Palace' – by which Shakespeare refers to Westminster (see Chapter 7). The Boar's Head Tavern makes an appearance in both plays. Established in the 1530s, this house of infamy stood for the best part of 300 years before the last of it was demolished in 1831. On today's Eastcheap, a 19th-century vinegar warehouse in the Venetian Gothic style stands on the site of the old tavern (at nos 33–35). The building is richly adorned with carvings by Robert Lewis Roumieu, including one of a boar's head which recalls the wild goings-on of centuries gone by. (*Tube: Monument*)

HENRY VI PART 1

Act 2, Scene 4 is set in Middle Temple Gardens. In a scene charged with both poetry and testosterone, Plantagenet and Warwick, Suffolk and Somerset swagger around and banter, picking roses to denote the battle lines of the coming conflict – white roses for Plantagenet and Warwick (the House of York), red for Suffolk and Somerset (the House of Lancaster). To this day Middle Temple Gardens are famed for their roses and open to the general public most lunchtimes. (*Tube: Temple*)

HENRY VI PART 2

King Henry VI deals with rebellion (as if he didn't have enough on his plate, what with macho nobles picking roses all over the place) at Blackheath. (*Rail: Blackheath*)

HENRY VI PART 3

The Battle of Barnet, in which Shakespeare cements the legend of Warwick the Kingmaker (see Chapter 4).

RICHARD III

The Tower of London (see Chapter 9), that statement of imperial might built by King William I, provides the backdrop for the bloody goings-on in Shakespeare's controversial (i.e. pro-Tudor) reading of the life of the king whom theatrical types delight in dubbing 'Dick the Shit' (Richard the Third = Richard the Turd… geddit?) Act 1, Scene 4 features two of the Bard's most memorable character names: First Murderer and Second Murderer. (*Tube: Tower Hill*)

HENRY VIII

By the banks of the River Thames, just a few metres along from Shakespeare's Globe going east, on a metal rail attached to the lip of the river wall, a quote from Act 4, Scene 2 of the drama that was playing when the first Globe burned down:

> *'Men's evil manners live in brass; their virtues*
> *We write in water.'*

Shakespeare's Globe Theatre

The current Globe has stood on Bankside since the 1990s and is the life's work of the American actor Sam Wanamaker. His dedication to having Shakespeare's theatre rebuilt slap-bang where it should be – that's London, where he wrote all of his plays, not Stratford, where he was born but never lifted a quill in dramatic anger – is a perfect parable for those who are feeling downcast about the world's lack of enthusiasm for a great idea. Despite the slings and arrows of red tape and bureaucracy, despite economic slumps and apathy, Sam Wanamaker achieved his goal of recreating a working, living monument to the Bard.

The theatrical practitioners at the Globe have long described the project as the best possible guess as to how the theatre would have been in Shakespeare's day. When new historical information comes to light, the folk at the Globe will try to factor it in. This refreshing approach translates to the stage as vibrancy – when the Globe players are in full spate, there is no more lively experience in town.

They also boast an architectural oddity in the first thatched roof to be permitted in London since the Great Fire in 1666 – at which event it was discovered that thatched roofs tend to burn really rather well. As such, they were outlawed until 1997, when special dispensation was made for the Globe.*

(*Pedant's corner: At the time of writing, the thatched roof on the Globe is actually the *second* to be permitted since 1666: the Globe was re-thatched a couple of years ago.)

In 2003, a gala was staged here in aid of The Prince's Trust. In attendance were the Prince of Wales and Camilla Parker Bowles (not quite yet the Duchess of Cornwall), entertained by, among others, Gwyneth Paltrow, Joseph Fiennes and Julian Glover, whose King Lear was such a monumental part of the 2003 season at the Globe.

Queen Elizabeth II opened the new Globe on 12 June 1997.

Winchester Palace (3)

Between 1529 and 1530, Thomas Wolsey – the famous Cardinal Wolsey, star and then pariah of Henry's inner circle – held the post of Administrator (or Bishop) of Winchester. Winchester Palace was the residence of the Bishops of Winchester for five centuries from the early 1100s. As such it has strong royal links – and not only to the English court.

In 1424 the captive King of Scotland James I (detained in England by Kings Henry IV and V for 18 years) held his wedding reception at Winchester Palace – by which point he was less a captive and more a guest at Henry V's court… only a guest who wasn't allowed to leave until Harry Five said so. His bride, Joan Beaufort, was the niece of the Bishop of Winchester.

One flake of the palace survives – an impressive 14th-century rose window. It can be viewed from Winchester Walk or the ravine-like Clink Street (so named for the infamous prison that stood there). Most of the palace burned down in 1814, but the rose window and the outline of the Great Hall still survive. For those of a gruesome turn of mind when it comes to leisure activities here in London, the Clink Museum stands on the site today.

King Henry VIII is thought to have first met fifth wife Catherine Howard at Winchester Palace in 1540.

The six-times-married monarch was also the subject of the last play staged at the original Globe Theatre on Bankside. *The Famous History of the Life of King Henry the Eight* (sic) had only been performed on two or three occasions when, in 1613, a stray spark from a cannon quite literally brought the house down.

Honor Oak (4)

Rail: Honor Oak Park

That this suburb of South London should take its name from a tree is no surprise given the leafy surroundings. And it is indeed a pleasant stroll up One Tree Hill – there are steps to the summit – to find the source of the name.

The Honor Oak in question marked the spot of a picnic taken on May Day 1602 by Queen Elizabeth I in the company of courtier Sir Richard Bulkeley of Beaumaris. The tree became known as the Oak of Honor to commemorate the royal occasion.

The tree that can be seen at the spot today, surrounded by protective railings, was planted in 1905.

The nearby beacon also has royal connections. It was placed there in 1935 to mark the Silver Jubilee of King George V and was lit to mark the jubilees – silver and golden – of Queen Elizabeth II.

Less than five miles from London Bridge, One Tree Hill is now a nature reserve.

Richmond Palace (5)

Old Palace Lane, Richmond TW9. Tube/Rail: Richmond

All that remains of the palace today can be seen between Richmond Green and the River Thames – the gatehouse dating from 1501, in red brick with the arms of King Henry VII featuring a crown, a shield with two quarters of three lions, and two of three Fleurs de Lys, the dragon of Wales and the greyhound of Richmond.

Upon the gatehouse, a plaque, doing as plaques do with their customary economical eloquence, records:

> *Richmond Palace*
> *A Residence*
> *Of*
> *King Henry VII*
> *King Henry VIII*
> *Queen Elizabeth I*

The royal history of Richmond is a rich one indeed. King George III watched the transit of Venus from a specially commissioned royal observatory here in 1769. One legend has it that King Henry VIII established what is now the protected view of St Paul's because he wanted to watch hunting (the view was protected from the establishment of the 'new' St Paul's in 1710 and allows for a clear view plus 'a dome-and-a-half' clear space either side of the cathedral).

From the Hammer of the Scots to the Virgin Queen, traces of regality abound. It was King Edward I who moved his court to a manor house at Sheen (1299), where he made the Scots grovel in the aftermath of the execution of William Wallace. His son, King Edward II, following his escape from the Battle of Bannockburn, founded a Carmelite monastery nearby, and his son, King Edward III, granted the manor to his mother Isabella. King Richard II made it his main residence, but then had it torn down upon the death of his wife, Anne of Bohemia.

King Henry VII built a palace there from 1500 (after an earlier palace on the site had burned down with the Royal Family in residence) and named it in honour of his earldom – Richmond.

Pause for breath.

King Henry VIII celebrated a lavish Christmas at Richmond with Catherine of Aragon in 1509. Queen Mary I resided at Richmond and held the future Queen Elizabeth prisoner here – which didn't seem to put Liz off the old place as she lived and died here.

James I preferred town and gave the palace to Prince Charles – later King Charles I – who established 'Richmond New Parke' and in 1625 kept clear of a plague here. The plague of 1625 enjoys an historical reputation that is a little less Hollywood than its younger brother of 1665, but I'm sure the symptoms were no less lethally unpleasant.

Ruination during the Commonwealth was the palace's sad fate. Parliament surveyed the place to see what it could yield in terms of raw materials and it was sold off for the grand sum of £13,000. King James II planned a restoration of the palace – to a design by Wren – but nothing came of it.

And so, to sum up, in the spirit of the Public Record Office (now known as the National Archives) at nearby Kew, here's a collection of Richmond Palace's royal hatches, matches and dispatches (the colloquial name given to the Public Record Office, where records of births, marriages and deaths are kept).

> **Births:** *one – Henry, Duke of Cornwall (Henry VIII's first son who lived for just 53 days in 1511)*
>
> **Marriages:** *two – Princess Margaret Tudor to James IV of Scotland (betrothal); Mary I (honeymooned here) with Philip II of Spain*
>
> **Deaths:** *three – Anne of Bohemia; King Henry VII; Queen Elizabeth I*

Crystal Palace (6)

Rail: Crystal Palace

Where the Great North Wood, a forest of oak trees, once stood, only the topographical vocabulary is verdant: Forest Hill, Woodside, Norwood. Legend has it that the trees at the highest spot – Upper Norwood today – were felled to build Francis Drake's *Golden Hinde*, the ship in which our great naval hero circumnavigated the globe between 1577 and 1580: only the wood closest to God was good enough for Drake.

From 1854 the Crystal Palace dominated the area. And despite the fact that the palace itself has been gone now some 80 years – destroyed by fire in 1936 – the neighbourhood where it stood is still popularly known by the Victorian nickname for the home of the Great Exhibition. Who would have thought that a building made primarily of glass would cast such a solid, long-lasting shadow?

Indeed, the impermanence of the building material goes very much against the grain of the Victorian age. All over London we have been left a legacy of Victorian architecture stamped with the institution or purpose for which the buildings were originally intended. St Pancras Station, for example, bears the crests of the long-defunct Midland Railway and symbols of that railway's destinations. Meanwhile, the General Lying-In Hospital near Waterloo will remain ever thus thanks to its name being etched into the stone.

It was as if that age could not countenance the notion that one day we might want to change or alter or even remove what these great Imperial Englishmen had set in stone. Did they view their Empire in the same way?

The Crystal Palace moved to South London after the end of the short lease on the Great Exhibition of 1851 site in Hyde Park. Sir Joseph Paxton's prefabricated glass and iron structure was rebuilt – and substantially redesigned in the process – in 1854. As she had in 1851, Queen Victoria performed the opening duties at the new site.

The works football team of the Crystal Palace Company grew into the modern-day Crystal Palace football team. The park was used as the venue for the FA Cup Final from 1895 to 1914, and it was at the last Crystal Palace final that King George V became the first reigning monarch to attend the famous fixture. He saw Burnley beat Liverpool by one goal to nil.

A different sport and a very different royal line was crossed at Crystal Palace in 1937 when Prince Bira of Siam raced in a Grand Prix here. Prince Bira is also, to this writer's knowledge, the only crown prince to die at a London Underground station. The Prince passed away in 1985 from heart failure at Barons Court station.

King's College Hospital (7)

Denmark Hill, SE5 9RS. Rail: Denmark Hill

Great history book euphemisms #1: 'It is said…'

This handy, catch-all phrase is deployed when the story about to be related lacks a certain amount of corroboration. And of Denmark Hill it is said that George of Denmark, consort of Queen Anne, owned a residence here in the shape of a large property on the east side of the hill.

The famous King's College Hospital – King's – was founded in 1840 as a training hospital for the students of King's College University. The king in question is King George IV, who founded the university in 1829 (with the Prime Minister, the Duke of Wellington) in the Church of England tradition, as a riposte to University College and its policy of educating people of all faiths and both sexes. The situation today is, of course, equality at all educational establishments.

King's College Hospital moved to Denmark Hill in 1909. Camilla Shand was born at the hospital in 1947. Later Camilla Parker Bowles, she is, of course, the current Duchess of Cornwall.

TEN ROYAL BIRTHS IN LONDON

Prince William
Will be the first king to have been born in a hospital – at St Mary's in Paddington in 1982. His brother Henry Charles Albert David (Harry to all the world) was born there two years later. The children of Anne, Princess Royal, were also born here: Zara in 1981 and Peter in 1977. Neither of the latter hold a royal title despite being 13th and 11th in line to the throne respectively.

Princess Beatrice and Princess Eugenie
Born at the Portland Hospital, a private facility on Great Portland Street, in 1988 and 1990 respectively. An illustrious place to enter the world, the princesses are in the company of the children of 50% of comedy double act French and Saunders, 20% of Oasis and 100% of the Spice Girls. Whether membership of Boujis comes as standard with the postnatal package, I have been unable to confirm.

Princess Victoria
Born at Kensington Palace in 1819 (see Chapter 1). At the time of her birth, she was fifth in line to the throne, but when her uncle, King William IV, died without

legitimate issue Victoria became queen. The equivalent leap up the queue today would be the ascension of Queen Beatrice I, although even to write such a thing may well be faintly treasonous.

George III
Born at Norfolk House, St James's Square. (Tube: St James's Park)

Anne, Princess Royal
The only one of Queen Elizabeth II's children not to be born at Buckingham Palace – she was born at Clarence House in 1950.

Queen Elizabeth II
Born Princess Elizabeth of York in 1926 and third in line to the throne (behind her father, who was behind his brother Edward VIII-to-be), she is the first monarch to be born in London since Edward VII in 1841 (at Buckingham Palace). Her birthplace, at 17 Bruton Street, Mayfair, was bombed in the Second World War.

Lambeth Palace (8)

Lambeth Palace Road, SE1 7JU. Tube: Lambeth North

Situated on the south bank of the River Thames, diagonally opposite the Houses of Parliament, Lambeth Palace is the official residence of the Archbishop of Canterbury. With the Abbey on the other side of Parliament to the west, the Methodist Central Hall at the Abbey's shoulder, and the Roman Catholic cathedral of Westminster loitering behind that, it's as if the Christian faiths are hanging around, seemingly casual-like, while keeping a watchful eye on proceedings at Westminster.

And at Lambeth they have had more need than most to keep an eye on government, particularly of the royal stripe.

The palace that we see today takes in many styles, due in part to its destruction by attack (the Peasants' Revolt of 1381), by neglect (during the Commonwealth) but not, unusually for an historic London building, by fire. The red-brick Tudor gatehouse dates from the late 1400s; the oldest part of the palace can be found in the chapel – the lower part of the east wall dating from around the early 13th Century.

Queen Elizabeth I is known to have stayed at the palace in 1593 and 1602. And it was at the self-same palace where the Earl of Essex was held prisoner after his abortive rebellion of 1601 – quite a comedown from the high jinks of the

ROYAL SOUTH LONDON

ROYAL LONDON

seditious staging of Shakespeare's *Richard II* just along the river at Southwark a short time before (see page 20).

Wimbledon

Tube/Rail: Wimbledon

Some parts of London have become a global byword for the businesses and spectacles that have made the areas famous – Fleet Street, for example, although all the newspapers have long left that fabled thoroughfare. Similarly the mere mention of the sedate London suburb of SW19 immediately serves up pictures of Pimms and strawberries and crisp white shorts, skirts and shirts.

In the time of King Edgar the Peaceful (a nice change to see a medieval king with an epithet other than 'the Bold', 'the Cross' or 'the Violent'), around 967 AD, the settlement was known as 'Wimbedounyng', meaning 'Wynnman's hill' – which has a pleasing ring of Henman Hill about it, the raised ground where British tennis fans have their hopes ritually dashed before a big screen.

The manor has been a royal possession on many occasions down through the centuries, being owned variously by Catherine Parr, Kings Henry VII and VIII, Mary I and Queen Henrietta.

The modern-day Royal Family has enjoyed a long association with Wimbledon through tennis. In 1929 Prince George (not to be confused with his elder brother, who would later become George VI) became president of the All England Club, a post taken over by his widow Princess Marina. Her son, the Duke of Kent, assumed the role in 1969 and, with the Duchess of Kent, is very much a fixture at the annual tennis jamboree.

In his role as president, the Duke of Kent (the Queen's cousin) made a change in etiquette at the famously traditional tennis tournament. From 2003 it has no longer been a requirement for the players to bow or curtsey to the royal box unless the occupants of said box are HM The Queen or HRH The Prince of Wales. The players passed the test of the new rule with flying colours when Her Majesty attended Wimbledon on 24 June 2010 – her first visit since 1977, when she watched Britain's Virginia Wade takes the Ladies' Singles title. The BBC reported that the Duke of Edinburgh has made more visits to Wimbledon than his wife – seven in all, to the Queen's four. In 2011, media attention concentrated on the recently wed Duke and Duchess of Cambridge.

The first royal visitor came not from England but from overseas when Crown Princess Stéphanie of Austria attended in 1895. King George V when

Prince of Wales began the House of Windsor's association with the old place, first attending in 1907. He was president of the Club until assuming the throne, when he became patron – a post inherited by each of his successors so far.

In 1926 Prince Albert (later Duke of York, later still King George VI, he of the now famous stutter) actually competed at Wimbledon. Partnering Louis Grieg in the Gentlemen's Doubles, our future king did the decent British thing and went out in the first round.

Eltham Palace (9)

Court Yard, Eltham, SE9 5QE. See www.english-heritage.org.uk/daysout/properties/ eltham-palace-and-gardens for prices and opening times. Rail: Eltham

Just as in Edinburgh, where the citizenry goes about its business in the presence of a castle atop a volcano, or in Rome, where the locals race around Roman ruins, the good folk of Eltham seem, on a day-to-day basis at least, to be unconcerned that they have a medieval palace in their midst.

In the early 14th Century the Bishop of Durham gave Eltham Palace to the man who would become King Edward II, who, in turn, gave it to his wife, Queen Isabella. King Henry VIII spent part of his childhood here, but the palace was eclipsed by the development of Greenwich as a royal residence.

The current house was built in the 1930s, incorporating what was left of the palace, which had, from the Civil War onwards, fallen into a deep decline. Today it is regarded as one of the best-preserved Art Deco interiors in the UK.

It is home to one of the greatest royal myths of them all: the origin of the highest order of chivalry in the land, the Order of the Garter.

The year is 1344. Or 1348. The Countess of Salisbury, Joan of Kent – or Catherine Montacute, her ex-mother-in-law (as you can see this legend already has confused origins) – is cutting a rug with King Edward III (for 'tis he) at Eltham Palace when her garter suddenly drops to the floor. Courtiers snigger at her medieval wardrobe malfunction (boys will be boys, as we have seen at Middle Temple Gardens earlier in this chapter) and, to save her blushes, King Ted steps forward, picks up the garter and pulls it onto his own leg, crying: 'Honi soit qui mal y pense' – 'Shamed be the person who thinks evil of it.'

A NICE SIT DOWN AND A CUP OF TEA

In the North, South, East and West chapters, where we cover a wider area of London, the places suggested to stop and have a cup of something reviving and a browse of this book may not necessarily be placed perfectly to strike out to see all the locations in one trip. They will be situated near at least one of our Royal London sites - and all will provide a warm welcome.

The wide open spaces of South London provide ample hospitality - both at 'the frontier' (the River Thames) and deep in the heartland.

On the main drag

Shakespeare's Globe

21 New Globe Walk, Bankside, SE1 9DT. Tube: Southwark

Being on the main drag is very much a stroke of luck for this great theatre - the original site was unavailable and a little less tourist-friendly. Here, it seems as if London has been built especially as a backdrop for the theatre.

Tea and coffee are available here even if you are not going in to see the play - although at £5 for a groundling ticket (available on the day) I would urge you to do so.

The coffee shop is open all year round, while the theatre itself closes from around October to April.

Something a little stronger, perhaps?

The George Inn

George Inn Yard, 77 Borough High Street, SE1 1NH. Tube: London Bridge

The last galleried coaching inn left in London, this great pub survives under the wing of English Heritage. So to have a glass or two here is to greatly benefit the cultural life of the nation. Do your bit. England expects!

Dickens refers to the George in Little Dorrit and Shakespeare's acting company, the King's Men, are said to have frequented the place. Further back still we have Chaucer connected with the area (his Pilgrims set off from the adjacent Tabard Inn). Great English beer on tap, food available, and a large courtyard for the summer months.

Sssshhh. It's a secret

Hop Scotch

72 Honor Oak Park, SE23 1DY. Rail: Honor Oak Park

Coffee shop by day, lively bar by night, if you're making the climb to the top of the hill then this independent outlet will work well at either end of the journey.

They even have live music on a Saturday. Perhaps you could put in a request for 'God Save the Queen' – either the national anthem or the Sex Pistols' version.

INTERREGNUM ONE
Ten persistent Royal London myths: all *not* true

Despite the fact that the history of the Royal Family has more wild and lurid tales than any soap opera could ever dream of, they are still not enough for some. Here are a few choice myths, retold one last time (I'm having my cake and eating it here, I know) so that we may now let them slip gently down the back of the sofa of history.

1. Edward III's garter fetish resulted in a chivalric order (see above).
2. Shenanigans at Middle Temple Gardens drew the battle lines for the Wars of the Roses. Great as the scene is… it never happened (see page 20).
3. Green Park is green because Catherine of Braganza had all the flowers removed to stop her husband King Charles II picking bouquets for his mistresses.
4. The male genital piercing known as the Prince Albert (no, I will *not* go into detail, thank you) takes its name from Prince Albert of Saxe-Coburg and Gotha, who himself was royally adorned with said item.
5. King Edward VIII invented the Windsor knot (it was his grandfather King Edward VII).
6. The Duke of Clarence was Jack the Ripper. He really wasn't.
7. King William III rode a powerful white charger like the Lone Ranger. Unlikely, this, as the King was only a few hands high himself.
8. James Hewitt is the father of Prince Harry. Hewitt has pointed out clearly, if a tad ungallantly, that the young Prince 'was already walking' by the time his affair with Diana began. Hard evidence for the persistence of the myth? Red hair, apparently.
9. William Wallace had an affair with Isabella of France and that, therefore, Edward III was not the son of King Edward II after all but of a Scottish freedom fighter/Australian actor. Isabella did not arrive in England

until 1308: Wallace had been chopped into four bits (five, if you include his head) in 1305. But then nobody ever said that *Braveheart* was a documentary.

10. There is no evidence to suggest that Queen Victoria ever uttered the line 'We are not amused.' Although perhaps she would have if Prince Albert really did have a big, rusty ring attached to his person.

3 ROYAL ST JAMES'S

Our favourite way to make our vast London seem more manageable is to imagine her as a series of villages. The royal village is the quarter known as St James's, whose 'boundaries' can be found at Haymarket to the east, Green Park to the west, St James's Park in the south and Piccadilly in the north.

For visitors it is in this part of town that royal history and pageantry can be seen to come alive in a 21st-century context. For lifelong Londoners such as your current correspondent, it can be easy to take it all for granted: there goes another parade – I hope it passes so I don't miss the no. 38 bus to Clapton Pond.

One of the great privileges of my work with London Walks, however, is seeing the pageantry through new eyes all the time: the eyes of London Walkers, citizens, denizens and visitors alike. For many of the people on my walking tours, the clip-clop of hooves and the rattle of carriages, the pomp and parp of brass bands and the flashing blue roar of motorbike outriders is not merely the background soundtrack of everyday life – it's the springboard for a thousand queries. Sometimes baffled, sometimes with an amused eyebrow raised, sometimes satirical (thanks largely to our dear Aussie friends!) Yet others query with an impressed reverence: 'What are they wearing?' 'Why are they stamping up and down from there to there?'

Similarly, the scale and grandeur of the architecture tells us that we're not in Kansas – nor, indeed, Kensal Green – any more. Again, the surroundings cease to become mere scenery as the questions mount up: 'Do people actually live in that house?' 'Can I buy a flag like that for my house back home?' 'Is the Queen at home?'

St James's Palace (1)

Cleveland Row, SW1A 1DH. Tube: Green Park

The senior royal palace. The original. The oldest palace in London still inhabited by the Royal Family (originally built between 1531 and 1536). Call it what you will, St James's Palace is still a big diplomatic deal even in the 21st Century – not least because (if you are reading this overseas) your ambassador to the UK is not the UK ambassador, but the Ambassador to the Court of St James.

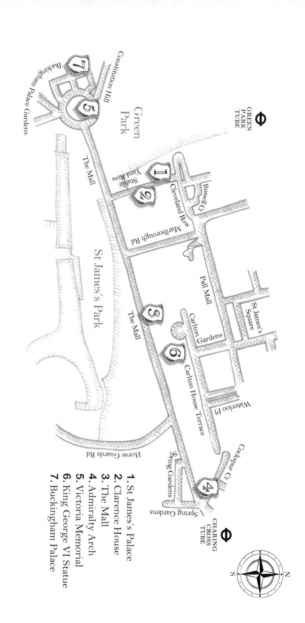

GREEN
PARK
TUBE
Φ

Constitution Hill

Buckingham Palace Gardens

7

Green
Park

5

The Mall

Stable Yard Row

1

2

Cleveland Row

Russell Ct

Marlborough Rd

Pall Mall

St James's Park

The Mall

3

St James's
Square

Carlton Gardens

6

Carlton House Terrace

Carlton Pl

Waterloo Pl

Horse Guards Rd

Spring Gardens

Cockspur Ct

Spring Gardens

4

CHARING
CROSS
TUBE
Φ

1. St James's Palace
2. Clarence House
3. The Mall
4. Admiralty Arch
5. Victoria Memorial
6. King George VI Statue
7. Buckingham Palace

N
S

The history of St James's Palace stretches back to its days as a hunting lodge in the reign of King Henry VIII and the fingerprints of our most celebrated royals can be found here.

King Charles I, having come second in the English Civil War (a silver medal really is worthless in this context) spent his last night on earth at St James's Palace in 1649 before making the short walk through to Whitehall where the axeman waiteth'd to reduce his height by about a foot or so – an adjustment that the King could ill afford, given that he was only 5 feet 3 inches tall to start with.

Legend has it that his faithful little dog trotted along with him every step of the way. His little dog trotted home alone.

Ernest Crofts paints a dignified king in his famous work of art 'King Charles I on His Way to Execution' (1883), in which the King walks tall (ahem) on this bitter January day towards his fate. Charles had taken the precaution of wrapping up warm to better resist the cold and not appear to be shivering with fear at his grisly destiny.

Charles II and his brother James II were both born at St James's Palace and Queen Victoria married Prince Albert of Saxe-Coburg and Gotha here in 1840. Anne Boleyn stayed here the night after her coronation. When dealing with the history of St James's Palace we really are dabbling in the Hollywood end of our story.

As discussed in the Kensington and West London chapters, red brick may not be the most regal of building materials (indeed Daniel Defoe once described St James's Palace as 'low and mean'), but then show is not the business here at St James's: business is the business here. St James's remains the official residence of the monarch. The official offices of Princes William and Harry are located at St James's Palace (although Harry's official res is Clarence House, more of that anon). The State Apartments are often used for important state visits of overseas dignitaries. The Royal Collection Department operates out of St James's too – they are the people in charge of opening the royal palaces to the public.

That taxis still career through between Pall Mall and The Mall, passing the eastern side of the palace, creates a similar feeling to the Roman spectacle of traffic raging around the Coliseum. The march of progress, powerful as it is, must break step and change direction to get around the truly great historical locations.

From the north, viewing the palace from Pall Mall, the gatehouse that stands today is a survivor of King Henry VIII's original palace (with the addition of Georgian windows and 19th-century clock). Resembling some red-brick rook from a vast chess set, with its octagonal towers either side of the pointed-arch gate, it calls to mind the Tower of London. And the architectural statement, I'm sure, is exactly the same: don't mess. Although a dwarf structure by today's standards, in the 1530s such a building would have cowed insurrectionist blood from a mile away. Having said that, the gatehouse retains a Tudor elegance that the brutish Tower of some 500 years earlier can only dream of. Red-uniformed sentries, adding a further delight for the snap-happy visitor, often guard the gatehouse.

GUARD-SPOTTING: HOW TO RECOGNISE THE REGIMENTS THAT GUARD THE ROYAL PALACES

As a tour guide, one of the most common questions I am asked about the guards is this: are they real soldiers? The answer is a solemn 'yes'. Were one to attempt to gain entry to the palaces or get too close to HM, one would soon discover just how real these soldiers are.

A YouTube video of a Scots Guard exacting physical revenge on a tourist who decided to send up the guardsman's march has clocked up more than a million hits – and a shocked reaction from visitors the world over. This shock was matched by the general British reaction that came down on the side of the harassed guard. The soldier was reprimanded for his conduct.

The second most popular question about the guards is which regiments do they belong to and how can you tell the difference if they all wear red tunics. Well, here's your handy cut-out-and-keep guide.

Regiment name	Plume in bearskin hat	Arrangement of buttons	Collar badge	Shoulder badge
Grenadier Guards	White	Single-spaced	Grenade	Royal crest
Coldstream Guards	Red	In twos	Garter star	Rose
Scots Guards	No plume	In threes	Thistle star	Thistle
Irish Guards	Blue	In fours	Shamrock	St Patrick star
Welsh Guards	Green and white	In fives	Leek	Leek

Clarence House (2)

The Mall, SW1 1BA. Tube: Green Park

When this writer was growing up, Clarence House was synonymous with one member of the Royal Family and one member only: the Queen Mother. As her official residence from 1953 until her death in 2002 at the age of 101, it was regularly the focus for TV news bulletins reporting on the landmark birthdays of this remarkable royal. Diana Spencer spent what she anticipated would be her last night as a single woman here – presumably the best counsellor for the experience ahead, that of Queen, was seen to be a woman who had not expected to take up the position herself yet had not only succeeded in but revelled in the role.

At the time of writing, Clarence House has become a byword for a different royal. When the news media report that Clarence House has issued a statement on, say, modern architecture in London, then they mean that His Royal Highness Prince Charles, the Prince of Wales, has something on his mind that he wishes to share.

The original structure was the work of John Nash, but the stuccoed, four-storey palace that can be seen today has been extensively remodelled, particularly in the post-war era. Viewing the palace from The Mall, the three feathers of the Prince of Wales can be clearly seen adorning the building despite the surrounding wall.

The new Duke and Duchess of Cambridge made their short hop to Clarence House after their buffet wedding reception with 650 guests, hosted by HM The Queen, with the Duke driving his father's convertible Aston Martin. The car had been a 21st birthday present to the Prince of Wales from the Queen.

The Mall (3)

Tube: Green Park/Piccadilly Circus/St James's Park

Like some immense red carpet – the brick-like hue of the road covering enhances the effect – The Mall is the great processional route that leads to Buckingham Palace.

And we love a parade here in Britain.

This love of spectacle can be indulged in London's most, well, spectacular office block, which serves as the entrance way to The Mall. Admiralty Arch **(4)** curves around the eastern end of The Mall, houses the Cabinet Office (since 2000, although plans are afoot at the time of writing to sell it off for £75 million) and was commissioned by King Edward VII to commemorate his mother – the inscription reads: 'In the tenth year of King Edward VII, to Queen Victoria, from most grateful citizens, 1910'. King Edward, alas, did not live to see its opening. We the public only see the opening of the central of the three gates on state occasions, but traffic rumbles through the adjacent arches all week.

Victoria bookends The Mall, with the lavish Victoria Memorial **(5)** at the other end of the route, just in front of Buckingham Palace. The architect that links the two is Aston Webb, designer of both Admiralty Arch and the vast plinth upon which Victoria's statue (by Sir Thomas Brock) sits – although plinth seems insubstantial a word for something made out of 2,300 tons of white marble.

This early 20th-century version of The Mall follows the line of the original route laid out from the 1660s. It takes its name (as does Pall Mall) from the game paille-maille, a cousin of croquet, which was popular at the court of King Charles II. The road that is modern-day Pall Mall is situated on the spot where the game was once played.

FOUR OF A KIND: FOUR QUEENS AND A KING KICKER ALONG THE MALL

Queen Victoria

The Victoria Memorial is the dot at the bottom of the great exclamation mark that is The Mall. Impressive on a smaller scale than the Albert Memorial, it is adorned with nautical references alluding to Britain's naval might (Britannia rules the waves and all that). Queen Victoria is kept company by four allegorical figures: the angels of Justice (looking to Green Park), Truth (her face turned Westminster-ward: think on, parliamentarians) and Charity (looking towards Buck Pal). The winged figure on top in gold is, of course, Victory.

Victoria herself watches the parades approaching from along The Mall. She may not look it, but I'm sure she is mightily amused by the pageant of British history unfolding.

Queen Alexandra

The Alexandra Monument is often overshadowed by Sir Alfred Gilbert's most famous London work – he also designed the figure we shall forever refer to as Eros at Piccadilly Circus. But his tribute to the wife of King Edward VII is no less impressive. Working in bronze on a red granite plinth, Gilbert gives us not a likeness of the late Queen, but an allegorical monarch, all-embracing, serene, benign, her cloak flowing around her subjects – represented by a child and two mournful attendants. The words 'Faith, Hope, Love' are listed as the Queen's virtues. The whole is topped off with the great Christian metaphor of light built into the structure with two street lamps in each upper corner.

Mary of Teck

The Queen who saw two of her sons and a granddaughter become monarch in her lifetime, and who was betrothed to not one but two Heirs Apparent, Queen Mary took up residence in Marlborough House in 1936. Her tribute in bronze can be found on the wall to The Mall side of this Christophers – plural, father and son – Wren structure.

The epically named Victoria Mary Augusta Louise Olga Pauline Claudine Agnes was born at Kensington Palace in 1867 and was first betrothed to the Duke of Clarence, eldest son of Edward VII. The Duke, however, died in the flu pandemic of 1891–1892, and in 1893 'May', as she was known, became engaged to the Duke of York (later King George V). Their marriage was a long and happy one and King George is said to have never taken a mistress. Like father unlike eldest son.

Queen Elizabeth

It always strikes me as a little sad that we only get around to casting bronze and shaping granite after a person is dead. Queen Elizabeth, the Queen Mother, with her eye for the theatrical (see the chapters on Westminster and East London), would have been, I'm convinced, particularly fond of her commemoration on The Mall. Elizabeth II unveiled the statue, by Philip Jackson, in February 2009 with the following words from HRH The Prince of Wales:

> 'All of us gathered here today will, I know, miss my darling grandmother's vitality, her interest in the lives of others, her unbounded courage and determination... her calm in the face of all adversity, her steadfast belief in the British people and, above all, her irresistible, irrepressible sense of mischievous humour.'

Cast in bronze at the base of the statue are depictions of the scenes from World War Two described in Chapter 6.

King George VI (6)

The statue of King George VI – standing lovingly at the shoulder of the Queen Mother today – was moved to its current position in 2009. From 1955 it had occupied the spot now taken by the Queen Mum. In the words of Prince Charles in February 2009:

> 'At long last my grandparents are reunited in this joint symbol, which in particular reminds us of all they stood for and meant to so many during the darkest days this country has ever faced.'

With the release of the Oscar-winning movie The King's Speech *in 2010, the pair gained wider recognition as a couple at last. Until this point, King George VI had been rather upstaged in the imaginations of our scriptwriting community by the fireworks of his elder brother King Edward VIII. It is perhaps appropriate that it was a film that allowed a new generation to appraise the life of our 'accidental' king: George and Elizabeth were avid movie fans. They had a cinema installed at Balmoral and instituted the Royal Command Film Performance. The first one took place at the Empire Cinema, Leicester Square, in 1946 with a screening of* A Matter of Life and Death, *a film by Michael Powell and Emeric Pressburger and starring David Niven.*

The statue is the work of William McMillan.

Buckingham Palace (7)

Buckingham Palace, SW1A 1AA. Tube: Green Park/Victoria

When we British indulge our love of understatement by referring to the monarch's primary residence as Buck 'ouse, our joke is closer to the truth than perhaps we think. From 1705 Buckingham House was the townhouse of the Duke of Buckingham – the current palace is built around that townhouse and has emerged in stages since the 19th Century.

Let's begin with the numbers: 775 rooms including… 19 state rooms, 52 royal and guest bedrooms, 188 staff bedrooms, 92 offices and 78 bathrooms. A double-glazing salesman's dream, a window cleaner's nightmare.

The palace remains a focal point for many a visit to London, and could also be described as A Very British Building Project – given that it was late and over budget. The cost of John Nash's original ambitious designs ran out of control and he was removed from the project in 1829, to be replaced by Edward Blore.

Queen Victoria became the first monarch to take up residence there in 1837 – and her infamous description of the building as 'my London slum' is perhaps down to the reining in of Nash's spirallingly ambitious plans. The chimneys smoked excessively and ventilation was poor in the extreme. So much so that when gas lighting was proposed there was a genuine concern that its installation would result in Guy Fawkes's seditious ambitions finally being brought to pass.

The 'front' of the palace as we know it today (actually the east wing) was originally designed by Blore and finally remodelled in 1913 by (that man again)

Aston Webb. Thus the evolution of the most famous royal palace has been almost as labyrinthine as the dynastic tale of the residents themselves.

As we view the palace from the Victoria Memorial, the most famous piece of the white Portland stone façade must surely be the balcony…

BALCONY SCENES

- Queen Victoria started the tradition of royal appearances on the balcony to celebrate the opening of the Great Exhibition in 1851.
- King George VI began the tradition of the RAF fly-past at the culmination of the Trooping of the Colour. The Royal Family watch the fly-past from the balcony.
- The newly wed Duke and Duchess of York took centre stage on the balcony on 23 July 1986 – and treated the crowds below to a pantomime spectacle, teasing the well-wishers over the much anticipated 'First Royal Kiss on the Balcony'.
- The 'First Royal Kiss on the Balcony' has only been a 'tradition' since 1981 – it was established by the Prince and Princess of Wales, Charles and Diana.
- In 2011, with the cameras of the world looking on, a bashful Prince William could be seen to mouth the words 'Shall we kiss?' to his new bride, who duly obliged. They both must have approved of the kiss, because a second one was attempted soon after. Although opinion in some quarters was that the kiss was too short. Some people are never happy!
- Winston Churchill joined King George VI, Queen Elizabeth, Princess Elizabeth (in the uniform of the Auxiliary Territorial Service) and Princess Margaret on 14 May 1945 to acknowledge the crowds at the end of the war in Europe.
- The ceremonial fly-past on Coronation Day, Saturday 2 June 1953, was almost cancelled due to bad weather. The young Prince Charles and Princess Anne were in attendance, as was the Queen Mother – although she did not attend the coronation at Westminster Abbey.

BUCKINGHAM PALACE FIRSTS

- First monarch to live at Buckingham Palace was Queen Victoria.
- First monarch to die at Buckingham Palace was King Edward VII.
- King Edward VII was also the first monarch to be born at Buckingham Palace. (William IV was born at the palace's predecessor, Buckingham House.)

- First electric lights at the palace –1883 in the ballroom.
- First man to be received at the palace in a lounge suit – Labour Prime Minister Ramsay MacDonald in 1924.
- The palace was first opened to the public in 1993 and within a week of booking opening, all group tours were booked for three years in advance.
- First café opened at Buckingham Palace in July 2010, selling refreshments to the 400,000 or so visitors that come through the palace every August and September. (The 2011 figures reached 600,000, thanks to the exhibition of the Duchess of Cambridge's wedding dress.)
- First jazz concert at the palace – by the Original Dixieland Jazz Band – took place as a Royal Command Performance in 1919 at the behest of King George V.
- First garden parties at the palace were held in the 1860s by Queen Victoria.
- First person to smoke a marijuana joint in Buckingham Palace was… well, it wasn't John Lennon. Nor was it any of the other Beatles. The persistent myth that The Beatles smoked dope at Buckingham Palace remains exactly that: a myth. Paul McCartney (now Sir Paul, of course) has speculated that, as all four Beatles were nervous when being presented with their MBE medals in 1965, they may well have had a cigarette in one of the 78 palace loos to calm the nerves. And with the passage of time (and, dare I say it, the number of subsequent joints smoked) the cigarette becomes a reefer and a legend is born.

These days when the Queen is in residence at Buckingham Palace, the Royal Standard flies. This flag is divided into quarters: the three lions passant guardant of England in the upper hoist and lower fly, the harp of Ireland in the lower hoist and the lion rampant of Scotland in the upper fly.

When flown in Scotland, the Royal Standard has lions rampant in the quarters occupied by the lions passant guardant when the flag is flown in England and vice versa.

SOME HERALDIC JARGON
Hoist: *the left-hand side of the flag, the bit attached to the pole.*
Fly: *the right-hand side of the flag, the bit furthest from the pole.*
Passant guardant: *an heraldic 'attitude', meaning striding from right to left facing directly outward (i.e. towards the viewer).*
Rampant: *up on hind legs, forepaws raised, head facing to the left of the flag.*

Motto: *from the Italian word for 'pledge', it is the heraldic mission statement of the coat of arms. 'Ich Dien' (German for 'I serve'); the Queen's crest has both 'Dieu et mon droit' ('God and My Right') and 'Honi soit qui mal y pense' ('Shame to him who evil thinks' – the motto of the Order of the Garter).*

Supporter: *figures on either side of a shield seeming to hold it up. The Queen's supporters are a lion and a unicorn.*

Escutcheon: *a shield.*

Field: *the background of a shield.*

Lozenge: *diamond shape on a field.*

Charges: *any emblems placed on the field.*

So… With the three lions passant guardant in the upper hoist and lower fly, the lion rampant in the upper fly and the harp in the lower hoist, the Royal Standard flies above Buckingham Palace when the monarch is in residence.

When the Queen is away from Buckingham Palace, the Union Flag is flown in her absence. In the event of a great tragedy, the Union Flag can fly at half-mast – as was the case on 9/11 for instance.

TEN UNORTHODOX PALACE VISITORS

Brian May

Buckingham Palace has seen enough exoticism in its history to render even the most outlandish and famous visitor merely commonplace. But it remains a fairly comment-worthy occasion when a legendary rock guitarist stands on top of one's house (this goes for any house, of course), strutting his plank-spanking stuff. But such was the spectacle in 2002 at the celebrations for Her Majesty's Golden Jubilee. I still think he might have worn a tie for the occasion, but the event was jolly good fun nonetheless.

Michael Fagan

Known forever as the Buckingham Palace Intruder, Fagan gained access to the Queen's bedroom, chatted to Her Majesty for a full 10 minutes, sitting on her bed, before asking for a fag. HM, cool as a cucumber, summoned a footman who then restrained the uninvited guest until the police arrived. Not only was Mr Fagan tie-less (he wore a T-shirt) but he was also barefoot. Which is also a sartorial no-no in the presence of royalty.

Gordon Brown, John Major*, James Callaghan, Harold Macmillan* and Sir Alec Douglas-Home
Five prime ministers who have gone to the palace for weekly audiences with the Queen despite not having secured the settled will of the people via an election. All five wore ties.
(*The two asterisked PMs went on to secure a mandate at the ballot box having succeeded to the premiership by becoming leader of the Conservative Party.)

Three campers
In 1981 three German tourists pitched camp in the grounds of Buckingham Palace believing it to be Hyde Park. Can be forgiven for not wearing ties as this would be absurd when camping, even in the grounds of Buckingham Palace.

FIVE INTERIOR 'STUNT DOUBLES' FOR BUCKINGHAM PALACE
Nobody, but nobody, films inside Buckingham Palace. The following buildings have become movie stars passing themselves off as the palace...

The King's Speech *(2010)*
Oscar-winning royal biopic has Lancaster House playing the part of Buckingham Palace. Now part of the Foreign and Commonwealth Office, it was once within the environs of St James's Palace.

Help! *(1965)*
The Beatles second cinematic romp sees Cliveden House stand in for Buckingham Palace. Cliveden House was once the estate of Frederick Prince of Wales, father of George III, son of George II, but never king. You can get to Cliveden (it's in nearby Berkshire) by train from Paddington; the journey takes about half an hour.

The Queen *(2006)*
Brocket Hall in Welwyn Garden City is the less celebrated star of this picture, standing in for Buck Pal. (There are trains to Welwyn Garden City from King's Cross.)

Young Victoria *(2009)*
Lancaster House again playing 'my London slum' (see page 42). As a by the by, Ham House down Richmond way is the stand-in for Kensington Palace.

King Ralph *(1991)*

Hollywood hokum with the unusual combo of John Goodman and Peter O'Toole making the whole thing more endearing than it should be. Upon the death of the entire Royal Family, uncouth Yank John Goodman (Ralph) becomes king. You can imagine the rest. Apsley House (Hyde Park Corner tube) is one of the stand-ins for the palace.

FIVE CAMEO EXTERIORS IN THE MOVIES

With the correct permits and permissions, Buckingham Palace can be featured from the outside on screen. The following are good examples...

Die Another Day *(2002)*

Toby Stephens as megalomaniac villain Gustav Graves does as megalomaniac villains are wont to do and announces his plan for world domination in front of Buckingham Palace.

101 Dalmatians *(1996)*

The Victoria Memorial can be clearly seen in the background of the chase sequence in the live action version of 101 Dalmatians that results in Joely Richardson and Jeff Daniels... oh, hang on, I don't want to spoil the plot if you haven't seen it.

The Prisoner *(1967)*

Not a movie per se, but the cult 1960s TV series did feature Patrick McGoohan speeding along The Mall in the famous opening credits.

National Treasure: Book of Secrets *(2007)*

Nicolas Cage action-adventure flick – in which Lancaster House also features, this time as itself!

Mamma Mia! *(2008)*

The quintessential Englishness of Colin Firth's character is established by him roaring through Admiralty Arch in a sports car heading towards Buckingham Palace – both in the movie and career-wise with The King's Speech just a short way off. (I am indebted to my London Walks colleague the movie expert Richard Burnip, or Richard IV as we call him, for help with the above lists.)

ROYAL ST JAMES'S

ROYAL LONDON

CHANGING THE GUARD

I often think that the rest of the world must look in on us here in London with our fondness for pageantry and mutter to themselves: 'What on earth are they up to *now*?'

But for every ceremony and parade, there is usually a good reason behind the whole affair. One assumes that the point here is visibility: don't mess with the monarch, she (or he) is heavily guarded.

Boiled down to its bare bones, Changing the Guard is simply one group of fellas heading off to work while another group of fellas pass them on the way home. Only most of us don't get a big brass band following us as we clock on and off.

While you watch the band it is worth checking out the various attitudes of your fellow spectators. Gentlemen of a certain age stand that little bit straighter at the stirring oompah of the musicians; visitors laugh and smile; a thousand digital cameras click synthetically as the red uniforms are captured as proof for the folks back home: 'Look! They really *do* march up and down dressed up in costume!'

Times vary depending on the time of year, so do check at www.changing-the-guard.com for confirmation of seasonal schedules.

BUCKINGHAM PALACE IN NUMBERS

- *800 – number of staff working at the palace. Two of them are horological conservators responsible for winding up the clocks.*
- *350 – number of clocks at the palace (see above).*
- *40,000 – number of light bulbs.*
- *1,514 doors (and 760 windows).*
- *40 – acreage of the gardens (featuring a helicopter landing area, a lake and a tennis court).*
- *600 – number of guests the Buckingham Palace kitchen is capable of serving at one sitting.*
- *9 – number of direct hits taken by the palace from Luftwaffe bombs during World War Two.*
- *3 – number of garden parties per year.*
- *27,000 – roughly the number of cups of tea served at a garden party.*
- *One – word the Queen uses when referring to herself in the first person singular.*

A NICE SIT DOWN AND A CUP OF TEA

It will come as no surprise, I'm sure, that there are many private members' clubs right in the heart of Royal London. If you are familiar with a member of, say, the Athenaeum or the Reform Club, my advice is to sweet-talk them into getting you in so that you may peruse this book in a balloon-back armchair with a bone china cup of Earl Grey to hand.

Coming up a blank on that front? Yes, me too. But there are still tea-related thrills aplenty to be had here in St James's...

On the main drag

The Garden Café

West Terrace, Buckingham Palace, SW1A 1AA. Tube: St James's Park

Not just 'on the main drag' - actually inside Buckingham Palace. Okay, the monarch isn't just going to let you drop in for a cuppa and a bit of a gossip about constitutional affairs. The Garden Café is open when the state rooms are open to the public - usually in the months of August and September, but check with the palace before visiting (www. royalcollection.org.uk). Teas, coffees, cakes and sandwiches, ideal for your own small-scale garden party. Last admission is 6.15pm at the time of writing.

Something a little stronger, perhaps?

Two Chairmen

39 Dartmouth Street, SW1H 9BP. Tube: St James's Park

Friendly pub, a little off the beaten track, but still popular with Westminster professional types at close of play – your journey to the pub from St James's station will take you past a statue of Queen Anne and some exquisitely preserved architecture from the period of her reign.

Sssshhh. It's a secret

Duke's Hotel

St James's Place, SW1A 1NY. Tube: St James's Park

Tucked away discreetly (very St James's) is one of London's most exclusive hotels. Offers a wide range of upmarket dining and drinking options including the Cognac and Cigar Garden. It was at Duke's where Diana, Princess of Wales heard the news of the finalisation of her divorce.

4 ROYAL NORTH LONDON

The fabled bendy blue frontier of London's River Thames – well, it's coloured blue on the maps at least – is the dividing line that defines the everyday lives of many a Londoner. Especially those who are trying to grab a late-night cab to head for the hills – the distant Muswell (north) and Forest (south) variety.

When looking for royal history north of the river, the first thought that strikes the visitor interested in royal landmarks is this: 'I seem to have discovered the spiritual home of the British republican.' Royal fingerprints from the modern era – that is the two centuries since the start of Queen Victoria's reign – are few and far between north of the river.

What conclusions can we draw from this? Is Hampstead really the 'nest of reds' that many a right-wing commentator would have us fear? Does Camilla, Duchess of Cornwall, have the born Sarf Londoner's aversion to Norf London? Is it because Prince William, famously an Aston Villa supporter, will only come to North London for football matches at Spurs or Arsenal? Or can we find an antipathy to the 'ordinary' people who live in such northerly enclaves as Tottenham?

I tend to think none of the above. Rather it is this: the common, everyday practices of the modern-day royals were set down in the 19th Century, particularly during the reign of Queen Victoria. By this point, the royal residences that we know and love today were already well established. Queen Elizabeth II also established many traditions early in her long reign – Sandringham in Norfolk for New Year being a good example. The royal story of the 19th and 20th Centuries has very much been one of consolidation in a time of great imperial upheaval. Little new ground – literal ground – has been broken in London in this period.

During the time of Diana, Princess of Wales we saw glimmers of a more modern approach. And much talk of a new era surrounded the wedding of Prince William and Catherine Middleton. Not only that, but HRH The Prince of Wales, as we shall see later in this chapter, has responded in a most modern fashion to 21st-century social upheaval right here in North London.

What all this does leave us, however, is the tantalising and rewarding business of finding clues from the deeper past of the royal history of London. And those clues are plentiful and sometimes surprising, in both their tone and their location.

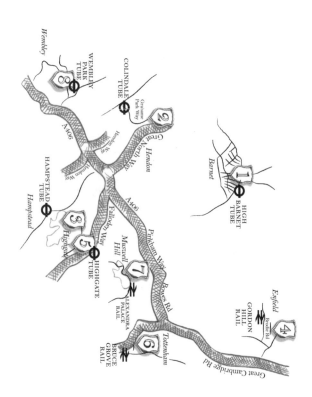

1. Barnet
2. RAF Hendon
3. Hampstead Heath
4. Brodie Road, Enfield
5. Highgate School
6. Bruce Castle
7. Alexandra Palace
8. Wembley Stadium

Barnet (1)

Tube: High Barnet

The Northern Line comes to a halt at Barnet – and so did the Wars of the Roses.

The Battle of Barnet (14 April 1471) proved to be a decisive blow in returning the Yorkist King Edward IV to the throne of England.

The Wars of the Roses in a nutshell? The great and storied dynastic conflict of English history that raged between 1455 and 1485, during which period the throne of England changed hands six times. The conflict takes its name from the emblems of the two sides, the red rose of Lancaster and the white rose of York – William Shakespeare uses broad poetic licence when setting the scene where each side selected their emblems, and places it at Middle Temple Gardens.

Battle commenced at Barnet early in the morning amid heavy fog. Cannon and arrows acted as a prelude to the bitter and barbarous hand-to-hand combat with swords and axes. The fog-addled fighting lasted from two to three hours and by its end some 1,500 men lay dead – the Earl of Warwick among them.

Warwick, popular among the people of England and once devoted to the Yorkist cause, had gained the nickname the Kingmaker and had been the leader of the Lancastrian forces.

In the spirit of the victors writing the history books, legend has it that Warwick was killed by the hand of Edward IV himself – a version that most historians reject. At the battle's end, Edward had issued orders to have Warwick captured alive – which remains the subject of great speculation. Did he want to win his former ally back to the Yorkist cause? Or did he have a lavishly gory public execution in mind for the traitor? In the spirit of this last, Edward had the naked corpse of Warwick and that of his brother, the 1st Marquess of Montagu, displayed for three days at St Paul's Cathedral to stamp out any potentially seditious cult growing around any legend of escape. Generally, the good folk at St Paul's these days frown upon such exhibitions, but the old place is still worth a visit. (The current St Paul's is, of course, only 300 years old, but the location remains the same.)

Warwick's legend was eventually secured, however, when Shakespeare (that man again) gave him some dramatic last words:

> *'Sweet rest his soul! Fly, lords, and save yourselves;*
> *For Warwick bids you all farewell to meet in heaven.'*

Unlikely, this, as being stabbed through the neck had finished him off.

Unfortunately for King Ted, he didn't get his own Shakespeare play. His brother, the Duke of Gloucester, did, and one with a starring role at that: Richard III. Perhaps King Ted didn't have a very good agent.

All of which seems a million miles from the villagey Englishness of Barnet today. Yet only half a mile or so separates this Costa Coffee-d, WH Smith-ed suburban High Street from the scene of the barbarism. Today, you'll find homes and a golf course – a battle being even more a spoliation of a good walk than a round at 'the gowf' – on the approximate location. But, since 1740, the Hadley Highstone has commemorated the Kingmaker's death. It currently stands on the Great North Road about 180 metres away from its original spot. The inscription on the obelisk reads thus:

> *Here was fought the famous battle between Edward IV and the Earl of Warwick April 14th Anno 1471 in which the Earl was Defeated and Slain.*

RAF Hendon (2)

Grahame Park Way, NW9 5LL. Museum open 10am–6pm daily. Admission free. Tube: Colindale

In the early 21st Century the flight requirements of the Royal Family are catered for at RAF Northolt. Hendon, however, retains its place centre stage when the popular imagination turns to all matters RAF, although this is thanks in no small part to the excellent RAF museum based there.

The King's Flight (the world's first fleet of aircraft dedicated to a head of state) was established at Hendon in 1936. It was later moved to RAF Northolt and was the subject of a news item in the *Independent* on 12 April 2006 when it was reported that: 'Tony Blair, Gordon Brown and ministerial colleagues were last night accused of using private jets in the Queen's Flight like a private taxi service.' The New Labour high-fliers denied the claim strenuously, despite the figures claiming that the Prime Minister used the Queen's Flight up to 60 times a year, whereas HM used it 'six or seven' times.

King George V was an early flight enthusiast, as had been his father King Edward VII, who had met the Wright Brothers and watched a demonstration of their aircraft in action.

An enthusiast he may have been, but when King George V found out that his son and heir (the man who would, briefly, be King Edward VIII) had flown in 1918 with a pilot who had one arm in a sling, he decided that it was best to clip the Prince's wings lest the nation lose a future king to the reckless pursuit of pleasure – a measure that proved, ultimately, futile.

The Prince of Wales later took delivery of a Gipsy Moth biplane in 1929, and from 1930 he and his brother – the man who would be king after the man who would be king – the Duke of York, later King George VI, father of Elizabeth II (I do hope you are paying attention at the back) – kept their aircraft at Hendon.

In December 1952 Prince Philip made the first solo flight by a member of the Royal Family in a helicopter. The model of helicopter was a de Havilland Chipmunk.

ROYALS WHO HAVE HELD RANK IN THE RAF
- *King Edward VIII – Air Marshal*
- *King George VI – Air Marshal*
- *Henry, Duke of Gloucester – Air Marshal*
- *Prince George, Duke of Kent – Group Captain*
- *HRH Prince Philip – Air Marshal*
- *HRH Prince Charles, Prince of Wales – Air Chief Marshall*

Hampstead Heath (3)

Tube: Hampstead; Rail: Hampstead Heath

Abandon hope all ye who cross the Heath – hope of navigating your way by street sign, that is. The Heath is free of the aesthetic pollution of 'signage' and is as delightful a place to get lost as London can afford. It also provides us with one of this book's earliest royal references: the land was granted to St Peter's monastery by King Ethelred the Unready in 986 AD.

As resistant to royal history as Hampstead seems at first glance, since 1992 it has been possible to visit the Queen at Hampstead Town Hall, 213 Haverstock Hill, NW3 – in the persona of MP for Hampstead and Kilburn Glenda Jackson.

By the time the next general election rolls around, the former actress Glenda Jackson will have represented her constituents in Parliament for two decades. And she is probably roundly sick of being described as an actress. But her status as such in the popular imagination is cemented by her legendary performance in the role of Queen Elizabeth I in the landmark 1971 BBC drama *Elizabeth R*, in addition to her two Oscars.

Brodie Road, Enfield (4)

Rail: Gordon Hill; Tube: Cockfosters

As ordinary North London streets go, Brodie Road is about as ordinary as they get. Early- to mid-20th-century villas and terraced housing in a variety of styles, quiet for the most part. Certainly not a typical haunt of dashing playboy princes – no offence, Enfield.

Yet the man who reigned over us, not so happy or glorious, as King Edward VIII has left his signature on this Enfield street in the shape of one of only 161 bright-red post boxes commissioned during his reign.

British mailboxes bear the name of the monarch during whose reign they were commissioned – VR for Queen Victoria, E VII R (Edward VII), a simple GR for King George V (there was no postal system as we recognise it today during the reigns of Kings George I–IV), G VI R (George VI) and, of course, E II R for Elizabeth II.

During the short, uncrowned reign of King Edward VIII – a mere 326 days – just 161 new post or pillar boxes, were commissioned. And one such example can be found in Brodie Road, Enfield, just along from the junction with Browning Road.

Letters form a central part of the legend of Edward VIII – not least his famous abdication letter, or 'instrument of abdication' as it was dubbed. In 2001, over 200 letters penned by the then Prince of Wales to his lover Freda Dudley Ward fetched £34,500. At almost double the expected price, this marks our enduring fascination with this star-crossed royal. His lover was – wait for it – a married woman whom he first met in 1918. One exchange in the letters is most revealing:

> *'What a hopeless state the world is in just now and each day I long more and more to chuck in this job & be out of it & free for you sweetie: the more I think of it all the more certain I am that really... the day for Kings & Princes is past, monarchies are out of date.'*

This letter was written some 14 years before he ever clapped eyes on Wallis Simpson. At which point his relationship with Dudley Ward ended abruptly.

The letters are addressed from 'Backhouse SW', so I am making the assumption that they were not posted from Enfield, but if new information comes to light we'll publish an updated edition of this book forthwith.

Highgate School (5)

North Road, N6 4AY. Tube: Highgate

The red-brick, twisty and gnarly English Gothic structure of Highgate School dates from the Victorian era. But the school dates back to the reign of that other formidable, epoch-defining woman of English history, Queen Elizabeth I.

Good Queen Bess granted by charter permission for Sir Roger Cholmeley to found a free grammar school for boys in 1565. After a long history as a public school for boys only, Highgate School went co-ed in 2004.

Former pupils include Poet Laureate Sir John Betjeman (1906–1984). The poet laureate – a post that stretches back to ancient Greece – is a government-appointed poet to the nation and has been the prime minister's responsibility since 1790, but originally was a royal appointment. Betjeman succeeded C. Day-Lewis in 1972 and held the post until his death in 1984.

SELECTED POETS LAUREATE IN LONDON SINCE QUEEN VICTORIA

1843–1850: William Wordsworth
The only laureate not to have composed a word of verse in his official capacity. Lived at Cheapside by St Paul's.

1850–1892: Alfred Lord Tennyson
Longest-serving laureate, ennobled by Queen Victoria – the first writer to be so.

1913–1930: Robert Bridges
Trained as a doctor at St Bartholomew's Hospital (Tube: St Paul's/Barbican) and composed 'London Snow':
   Then boys I heard, as they went to school, calling,
   They gathered up the crystal manna to freeze
   Their tongues with tasting, their hands with snowballing;
   Or rioted in a drift, plunging up to the knees.

1930–1967: John Masefield
Wrote 'So many true Princesses who have gone', set to music for choir and orchestra by Edward Elgar for the unveiling of the Queen Alexandra Memorial outside St James's Palace (situated just off The Mall). (Tube: St James's Park)

1968–1972: Cecil Day-Lewis

English Heritage blue plaque on his former home at 6 Crooms Hill, Greenwich. (Rail/DLR: Greenwich)

1972–1984: Sir John Betjeman

A blue plaque can be found on his former home in Cloth Fair, EC1. (Tube: Barbican) Martin Jennings' statue at St Pancras station finds Betjeman gazing heavenward, as if struck by inspiration. Betjeman helped save the Gothic masterpiece of St Pancras from demolition in the 1960s.

1984–1998: Ted Hughes

Commemorated, but not re-interred, at Poets' Corner in Westminster Abbey in December 2011.

1999–2009: Andrew Motion

Born in London and raised in Essex, Motion is the first poet laureate to survive the post! Upon accepting the honour, Motion broke with tradition by announcing that he would stay on for ten years only.

Wrote 'Spring Wedding' in 2005 for the marriage of HRH The Prince of Wales and Camilla Parker Bowles.

2009: Carol Ann Duffy

The first openly gay poet, the first Scot, and the first woman to hold the post. Composed the poem '46 Rings' in honour of the marriage of Prince William and Catherine Middleton.

Tottenham Green Leisure Centre

1 Philip Lane N15 4JA. Tube/Rail: Tottenham Hale

In August 2011, HRH The Prince of Wales visited riot-torn Tottenham in the aftermath of the biggest civil upheaval seen in our country in decades. ITN later broadcast footage of Prince Charles as he was approached by a young rapper who offered the Prince a hip-hop CD. Introducing himself as an actor and a poet and a rapper, he suggested that more youth clubs would form part of the solution to modern society's ills, before presenting the Prince with his musical gift. 'It *is* reasonable rap, isn't it?' asked the Prince. 'Yeah, it's reasonable,' the young artist assured the royal visitor, adding, 'go home and have a listen, yeah?' before signing off with 'God bless ya Prince!' and a warm, matey pat on the royal arm.

Earlier, the Duchess of Cornwall (in the BBC footage) had been greeted by a cheery Tottenhamite with almost ambassadorial formality and a grin as wide as the Seven Sisters Road is long: 'Hello Camilla, how are you? Welcome to Tottenham.' The only anachronism was that he filmed the whole encounter on his mobile phone as he chatted.

In terms of just exactly how many breaches of royal protocol had been witnessed, statisticians are still rattling the abacuses and consulting dusty tomes at the time of going to press, but all involved – HRH, locals and media alike – emerged looking jolly and more than a little relieved that dialogue had been achieved in a week of great strife in our city's modern history.

The Prince's Trust announced an immediate £2.5 million investment in the hardest-hit areas following the riots.

Tottenham's royal history, however, stretches much further back than the early 21st Century.

Bruce Castle (6)

Lordship Lane, N17 8NU. Museum open Wed–Sun, 1pm–5pm. Rail: Bruce Grove

Fingerprints of the royal line of Scotland can be found here, too. The House of Bruce once owned much of the land. Upon his ascension to the Scottish throne in 1306 as King Robert I, Robert the Bruce forfeited all claims on his English lands.

Bruce Castle (only the name remains from the days of the Scottish king) as it stands today is a Grade I listed 16th-century structure. The oldest parts of the castle were built by William Compton. Compton, around a decade older than King Henry VIII, was a close confidant of the King and was appointed Groom of the Stool at the outset of Henry's reign. The Groom of the Stool was, as the name suggests, responsible for providing the means for the monarch to defecate in appropriately regal comfort by first fetching or arranging the provision of a commode (portable toilet) and then waiting in attendance for nature to take its course.

The historian Dr David Starkey points out that, although this seems a menial task to our modern sensibilities, the intimacy of the situation brought about unrivalled access to the king. A powerful position indeed.

King Henry VIII is known to have visited Bruce Castle and to have hunted in nearby Tottenham Wood. The fossils of Tottenham Wood are plain to see in the modern London name Wood Green, which has stood on the site of the old wood since urbanisation in the Victorian era.

The Bruce Castle that can be seen today is a red-brick structure – less castle, more manor house – laid out in an E-shape. A clock tower surmounts the central porch (the middle 'leg' of the E). The various alterations to the building create the effect of seeing the Jacobean past through the prism of the classicists.

The castle now plays host to a museum and houses the historical archives of the London Borough of Haringey. There's also a postal exhibit featuring – that topic again – historic pillar boxes, including an unusual example in blue (for air mail letters) with the lettering GR (see page 56).

Alexandra Palace (7)

Alexandra Palace Way, N22 7AY. Rail: Alexandra Palace

It is one of the great common modern misconceptions of Royal London that Alexandra Palace was the residence of the wife of King Edward VII. It's a simple mistake to make. Built in 1862 by the Great Northern Palace Company, the original name for the project was to have been the Palace of the People or the People's Palace. The decision was taken to rename the palace in honour of Alexandra of Denmark, who married the Prince of Wales in 1863.

Ally Pally, as it is affectionately known, is famous as the home of the world's first purpose-built high-definition TV studios. The first broadcasts in 1936 could only reach homes within a 35-mile radius of Ally Pally and only 20,000 of those homes were equipped with a set to receive the signal. Sets cost in the region of £100.

NINE HISTORIC ROYAL BROADCASTS (AND ONE FAMOUS NON-BROADCAST) FROM LONDON

1924: *King George V makes the inaugural radio broadcast by a monarch on the BBC from Wembley (see below) on 23 April.*

1934: *The first royal wedding broadcast from the BBC by radio. The Duke of Kent and Princess Marina marry at Westminster Abbey on 29 November.*

1937: *The coronation of King George VI and his Queen Consort Elizabeth, covered by a simultaneous radio and television broadcast. An outside broadcast van is used for the first time.*

1953: *Sales of television sets rocket and 20 million viewers around Europe watch the BBC broadcast of the entire coronation ceremony – featuring, for the very first time, the actual moment of coronation.*

1960: *HM The Queen's first Christmas broadcast is recorded at Buckingham Palace. Until this point, Sandringham had been the most popular recording place.*

1969: *HM The Queen decides against the traditional Christmas message, in the belief that the investiture of the Prince of Wales along with that year's TV documentary* The Royal Family *constituted something approaching overkill.*

1981: *Some 750 million people worldwide tune in to the wedding of Prince Charles and Lady Diana Spencer.*

1995: *15 million viewers watch Diana, Princess of Wales give her now infamous 'Three people in that marriage' interview with Martin Bashir for the BBC's* Panorama *programme. The frank and confessional 40-minute conversation includes an admission of adultery on Diana's part with her riding instructor James Hewitt.*

1997: *BBC announcer, 31 August: 'This is BBC Television from London. Normal programming has been suspended and we now join Martyn Lewis in the news studio…' Lewis: 'This is BBC Television from London. Diana, Princess of Wales has died after a car crash in Paris. The French government announced her death just before five o'clock this morning. Buckingham Palace confirmed the news shortly afterwards.'*

2011: *The wedding of Prince William and Kate Middleton generated a 2,400MW power surge in the UK as viewers at home – nearly 25 million of them – switched on their kettles for that immortal British curative in the aftermath of high excitement, a nice cup of tea.*

Wembley Stadium (8)

Wembley, HA9 0WS. Tube: Wembley Park

The first Wembley Stadium opened in April 1923 as the Empire Stadium and was home to the British Empire Exhibition of 1924. During the construction, the honour of cutting the first turf was given to no less an imperial hand than His Majesty George V, by the Grace of God, of the United Kingdom of Great Britain and Ireland and of the British Dominions beyond the Seas, King, Defender of the Faith, Emperor of India.

The stadium's legend lies principally in its association with the national game of football (soccer). The first game played there, just four days after it opened, kicked off on 28 April 1923: the FA Cup Final between Bolton and West Ham. The match was delayed by three-quarters of an hour because of the vast crowd in attendance: 126,047 is the official figure left for the history books although some sources estimate up to twice that number. The game has gone down in history as the White Horse Final; Billie, a white police horse, being instrumental in clearing the field of play to allow the game to commence and upstaging even guest of honour King George V. *The Times* opined that the arrival of the King, and an enthusiastic rendition of the national anthem, helped calm the crowd during an otherwise chaotic afternoon. Bolton Wanderers beat West Ham United by two goals to nil.

The next year, 1924, King George V made the first royal radio broadcast from the British Empire Exhibition – an exhibition 'to stimulate trade, strengthen bonds that bind mother country to her sister states and daughters, to bring into closer contact the one with each other, to enable all who owe allegiance to the British flag to meet on common ground and learn to know each other'. His broadcast was relayed to the nation not just by radio but also by loudspeakers outside major department stores through these islands. In places this spectacle was so popular that it stopped the traffic.

In 1948, on 29 July, the Summer Olympic Games opening ceremony took place in the presence of His Majesty King George VI, Queen Elizabeth and Queen Mary. At 4pm that afternoon, the King declared the Games – the first since 1936 – open.

The most famous sporting day in the history of the old stadium was the World Cup Final of 1966 on 30 July, when England defeated West Germany by four goals to two. England captain Bobby Moore famously wiped his battle-muddied hands before shaking the be-gloved hand of Her Majesty upon receipt of the trophy.

Queen Elizabeth II watched the match and was subject to something of a colour clash when presenting the medal to England goalkeeper Gordon Banks, resplendent as they both were in yellow. The Queen's official dressmaker in 1966 was Sir Hardy Amies – a post he held until his death in 1989. Widely regarded as the founding father of 'bespoke couture' – a radical hybrid in its day in stuffy, post-war Savile Row – Sir Hardy, through his equally radical populist crossover design deal with Hepworth's (parent company of today's High Street chain Next) also designed the blazers and leisurewear sported by the England football players in 1966.

The most famous non-sporting day in the history of the old stadium came on 13 July 1985 with the staging of the Live Aid concert in aid of famine relief in Ethiopia. Queen famously stole the show – not, in this case, Her Majesty, but the rock band fronted by Freddie Mercury.

The Prince and Princess of Wales were in attendance, accompanied into the royal box by the man behind the concert, Bob Geldof, to the royal fanfare played by the Coldstream Guards. The Prince nodded along to Status Quo with the air of an heir who would rather have been fishing on Royal Deeside. The Princess smiled politely like a gal who preferred Duran Duran.

Wembley Stadium was also used for the Diana memorial concert in 2007 – this time at the New Wembley. The famous twin towers of the 1923 edifice had been demolished in 2003 – much to the dismay of some traditionalists – and replaced with the 90,000-seater stadium (the second largest in Europe) that stands on the site today. Designed by Foster and Partners and Populous, the towers have been replaced by a skyline-defining arch 440 feet (133 metres) high with a span of more than 1,000 feet (315 metres).

It was beneath this unique London feature that the Concert for Diana was staged on 1 July 2007, on what would have been her 46th birthday, 10 years on from her death. The concert featured performances from, among many others, Diana favourites Sir Elton John and Duran Duran. Princes William and Harry, the organisers, addressed the fans at the sell-out concert. 'This evening is about all that our mother loved in life – her music, her dance, her charities and her family and friends. For us, this has been the most perfect way to remember and this is how she would want to be remembered.'

In a Boujis-Nightclub-Goes-to-Wembley-like scenario, also in attendance were Princess Beatrice of York, Princess Eugenie of York, Prince Harry's girl-friend Chelsy Davy and the future Duchess of Cambridge back in her days as 'Waity Katy' – at this point the girl who hung on for an age for a proposal out of our future king was filed under 'just friends' in William's Facebook status. Philippa Middleton was also there. Also in attendance (but not part of the Boujis set) were Zara and Peter Phillips, and Sarah, Duchess of York – the latter also not part of the Boujis set but perhaps not for the want of trying.

All proceeds from the concert went to charity.

A NICE SIT DOWN AND A CUP OF TEA

Three suggestions here in North London, each right at a location named in the chapter.

On the main drag

RAF Hendon

Grahame Park Way, NW9 5LL. Tube: Colindale

If you're up north on the trail of royal fliers (and, indeed, the Royal Air Force), then the cafeteria here at RAF Hendon provides a unique opportunity: where else can you sip tea surrounded by historic aircraft? The staff at the museum, on my last visit, were particularly helpful and friendly.

Something a little stronger, perhaps?

The Spaniards Inn

Spaniards Road, NW3 7JJ. Tube: Hampstead

The Spaniard's Inn dates from the 1580s and is said to take its name from the Spanish Ambassador to the court of King James I. The Spaniards feels warm inside and clandestine on a winter's day/night and has perhaps the most magnificent beer garden in all of London for the summer months. A bracing/thirst-making walk across the Heath will get you here (alternatively, the 210 bus will bring you almost to the door from Golders Green station). Good food, too.

Sssshhh. It's a secret

Bruce Castle Park
Tube: Wood Green/Seven Sisters

Far from secret to the local residents, Bruce Castle Park teems with things to do for local families in summertime. And it is dotted with picnic benches. It seems a shame not to linger when you've stumbled upon a rare 16th-century manor house deep in the heart of suburban London.

INTERREGNUM TWO

Ten royal assassination attempts, regicides, executions and/or kidnappings

The admirable restraint that is such a central feature of the British character is plain for all to see in the fact that we have assassinated only one of our prime ministers – Spencer Perceval in 1812.

GUY FAWKES

The most famous of them all and the one that we 'Remember, remember the fifth of November, gunpowder, treason and plot'. Tried to blow up King James I in 1605, failed and was executed for his trouble (see Chapter 9). In 2005 the British TV presenter Richard Hammond fronted the ITV programme *The Gunpowder Plot: Exploding the Legend*, which staged the explosion-that-never-was using 17th-century gunpowder and a costly reconstruction of the Palace of Westminster as it was in 1605. The show was viewed in some quarters as merely a blokey excuse to blow something up. The results of the experiment, however, revealed that Fawkes meant business. The walls of the palace – more than 2 metres thick – were reduced to rubble. Everyone within a 100-metre radius would have been killed instantly. Falling debris would have at least seriously injured anyone within a 400-metre radius.

QUEEN VICTORIA

In May 1842 one John Francis took aim with a pistol at Queen Victoria in her carriage as she rode along The Mall, but did not fire. The Queen repeated her journey the very next day, under heavy escort, to tempt the would-be assassin into the open once more. The plan succeeded – Francis fired, missed and was apprehended by plain clothes officers. His death sentence for high treason was commuted to penal transportation. Queen Victoria survived eight assassination attempts of varying degrees of competence.

KING GEORGE III

Subject of an unsuccessful assassination attempt when two pistol shots were fired at him while watching a play in Drury Lane.

KING EDWARD VIII

As if his brief reign wasn't dramatic enough, he was also the subject of an assassination attempt on 16 July 1936 at Constitution Hill.

ATTEMPTED KIDNAP OF PRINCESS ANNE

Six shots were fired and four people were wounded when the car carrying Princess Anne and her then-husband Captain Mark Phillips was forced to a halt by another vehicle. The unsuccessful kidnapper was one Ian Ball, who had written to the Queen demanding £3 million for the Princess's return. Among the offences for which he was tried was the attempted murder of the Princess's bodyguard.

ANNE BOLEYN

See Chapter 9.

KATHERINE HOWARD

See Chapter 9.

KING RICHARD II

Overthrown by Bolingbroke who became King Henry IV, Richard is thought to have been allowed to starve to death in captivity. His remains are interred at Westminster Abbey.

MARY, QUEEN OF SCOTS

See Chapter 7.

KING CHARLES I

Beheaded at the Banqueting House, Whitehall. Gruesome myths of 30 January 1649 abound. His followers, it is said, dipped their handkerchiefs in his blood –

no eyewitness account of this scene exists. Cromwell permitted the King's head to be stitched back onto the royal body, so that the family could pay their final respects. A black mark on the clock at Horse Guards Parade commemorates the hour of his death. The mark can still be seen today at the numeral II. The King's statue just to the south of Trafalgar Square marks the very centre of London.

5 ROYAL GREENWICH

Greenwich Park (1)

Greenwich, SE10. DLR: Cutty Sark/Greenwich. Rail: Maze Hill/Blackheath

First, a quick word about getting to Greenwich. Rail links are plentiful and easy to follow. The good folk of the Docklands Light Railway have even named one of their stations 'Cutty Sark for Maritime Greenwich' to make it easier.

But if you want to hit this old royal stamping ground in true regal style, the best way to do so is by boat.

Okay, the eastbound boats from Westminster and Tower piers may lack the decadence and sheer theatricality of a Tudor royal barge (no offence to the boat operators!) but they will provide the easiest way to follow the common royal route that was used right up until the middle of the 19th Century. King Henry VIII was born at Greenwich and would have used the water regularly to get along to Hampton Court way out west.

Thames Clippers run regular services on the Thames – with seasonal variations – and their website is at www.thamesclippers.com.

A boat trip along to Greenwich from Tower Hill is also a feature of London Walks' regular Greenwich tours.

In all of London, Greenwich provides perhaps the most harmonious blend of royal past and royal present. Its roots as a royal playground stretch back to the 1400s, but in this glorious corner of South-east London, history is far from hidden. The Royal Hospital, the Royal Observatory and the Royal Park all provide an impressive backdrop to a vibrant neighbourhood. To describe present-day Greenwich without using the word 'splendour' is as tall an order as describing a spiral staircase without using swirly hand gestures.

When it comes to Greenwich, or indeed the Royal Family, 'new' is seldom a word we throw around. Yet that's precisely what the old girl Greenwich is: the newest Royal Borough of London. The honour has been bestowed to celebrate the Diamond Jubilee of HM Queen Elizabeth II in 2012.

Greenwich is, of course, far from new. Its royal links go back around 600 years in this village. Not quite as old as the Abbey (see Chapter 7) of course, nor quite as old as time, even if time as we know it is as old as Greenwich.

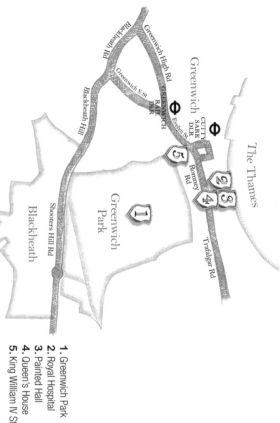

Blackheath Rd

Greenwich High Rd

Greenwich S St

Blackheath Hill

GREENWICH RAIL DLR

Evelyn St

Greenwich

CUTTY SARK DLR

Φ

Φ

The Thames

Romney Rd

⑤

②③

④

①

Greenwich Park

Shooters Hill Rd

Blackheath

Trafalgar Rd

1. Greenwich Park
2. Royal Hospital
3. Painted Hall
4. Queen's House
5. King William IV Statue

In terms of royal stars, all the big-hitters are here: King Henry VIII, King Charles II, Liz I and more. And the walk-on parts are pretty impressive, too: Nelson, Captain Cook, Christopher Wren are just the tip of the imperial iceberg. Factor in location – on the Thames, the gateway to the world and the path to empire building. Greenwich is where the land meets the water and its story is that of an empire that felt confident it had already tamed the former, and was keen to rule the latter in order to conquer more.

The Palace of Placentia

On the site of the Old Royal Naval College, King William Walk, SE10. Tube: Cutty Sark

That Greenwich became a Royal Borough in name in the year 2012 is a needless appellation for many. Greenwich has always been a royal borough, ever since King Henry VI's Lord Protector the Duke of Gloucester enclosed the 200-acre park here and commenced the building of an impressive palace in 1422.

Hitherto it had been a 'solitary wilderness', in the words of Geoffrey Chaucer. Humphrey, Duke of Gloucester – brother of Henry V – was very much a man of parts – military hero, skilled diplomat and academic. His book collection formed the basis of the hallowed Bodleian Library in Oxford.

He lacked the smarts, however, to notice that his wife Eleanor of Cobham got up everyone's noses with her fondness for astrology and potions, and when her astrologers predicted ill health for King Henry VI (Gloucester's nephew), the writing was on the wall. The astrologers were arrested on a charge of treasonable necromancy – not an offence one hears often down the Old Bailey these days – and executed. Eleanor was made to do public penance and divorce her husband, and was sent to prison for life. And how, pray, had King Henry VI found out that Eleanor's astrologers were lying? Why, he asked his own astrologers, of course. It's like a scene straight out of *Blackadder*.

Gloucester himself was had up for treason in 1477 but died three days after his arrest. Some say he was poisoned; others that he died of a stroke. I'm going to counsel that we err on the side of the stroke: we don't have to go looking for lurid deaths and conspiracy theories, given the larger-than-life figure who is looming just down the red carpet of our narrative…

Gloucester's Greenwich Palace, by then named Bella Court, became the possession of King Henry VI, and Henry's wife Margaret of Anjou had the ol' place beautified with terracotta tiles, the great luxury of glass in windows, a treasury and landing stage for sailing vessels. She renamed it Placentia, meaning Palace of Pleasures.

Which brings us to that aforementioned larger-than-life figure seldom noted for his ability to deny himself any Placentia whatsoever…

The popular image of King Henry VIII – that of the, er, big-boned wife de-capitator – will probably never be dislodged from the collective imagination. This despite the best efforts of racy TV dramas with lantern-jawed and ripe young actors in billowing shirts open to the waist (be still, my beating heart).

The truth of the matter exists somewhere between the two. Much as Queen Victoria wasn't always aged and tough to tickle (see Chapter 1), it follows that King Henry VIII wasn't always such a blimp. In his younger days the American-English expression 'jock' would very much fit the bill: sporty, active, competitive in the extreme.

Jousting. Shields. Tents. Heraldry. Those tall, pointy hats with the damask veil fluttering like a flag. Does anything say 'yore' like a tournament?

As a young man, Henry revelled in the thrill of the tournament. And his opponents were not necessarily always other sportsmen. Indeed, it was at just such a tournament at Greenwich in 1536 that his wife Anne Boleyn was arrested and taken to the Tower on a number of trumped-up charges so that Hank might move on and get down to the breath of fresh heir that was Jane Seymour.

In a brutal belt-and-braces approach, Henry had five men – including Anne Boleyn's own brother – arrested on charges of adultery with the Queen, incest and high treason. Anne and the five men were found guilty and duly executed. This gory fate befell them despite the fact that, for some observers and many historians, the cases against them didn't quite come off. Unlike Anne Boleyn's head (see Chapter 9).

Greenwich runs through the story of Henry VIII's life like veins through a slab of marble. He loved hawking and hunting in the park against the backdrop of ships bringing silk and gold and spices up the Thames.

It is thanks to Henry that we know the place as Maritime Greenwich (more of that anon), but it could just as easily be dubbed, in Henry's case, Marital Greenwich. We are so distracted by the catalogue of goings in his married life that sometimes we forget about the comings.

Henry was married thrice at Greenwich – first to Catherine of Aragon, his brother Arthur's widow. He later married Anne Boleyn here in secret in 1533. Oh, and Anne of Cleves, too. Are you keeping up? I'll put it in a handy list to go with the famous one about the six wives, the one that goes:

Divorced – Beheaded – Died
Divorced – Beheaded – Survived

In the same vein, the wedding venues go:

Greenwich – Greenwich – Whitehall
Greenwich – Oatlands Palace – Hampton Court

Was he giving Greenwich just one last chance before moving on? The marriage to Anne of Cleves was doomed from the start. Henry had never before met his bride and wasn't over-smitten by her looks (see quote 4, below).

SIX QUOTES FROM KING HENRY VIII ON HIS SIX WIVES
1) **Catherine of Aragon:** *'[My marriage is] blighted in the eyes of God.'*
2) **Anne Boleyn:** *'... to wish myself (specially an evening) in my sweetheart's arms, whose pretty ducks* I trust shortly to kiss.'*
   * Ducks = breasts
3) **Jane Seymour:** *This from his last will and testament: '... that the bones and body of his true and loving wife, queen Jane, be placed in his tomb.'*
4) **Anne of Cleves:** *'The ugliest woman in Christendom.'*
5) **Katherine Howard:** *'My rose without a thorn.'*
6) **Catherine Parr:** *'Most dearly and most entirely beloved wife.'*

Both of his daughters – Queen Mary I and Queen Elizabeth I – were born at Greenwich, too. In January of 1536 Anne Boleyn delivered a stillborn son at Greenwich early in her labour. It is said that her travails were brought on after discovering her Henry unable to wait for her lady-in-waiting Jane Seymour.

Henry's sickly son and heir Edward VI died at the palace in July 1553, aged just 15.

The Tudor king's royal footprint spreads wider than modern-day Greenwich: a little further along the water at Deptford, he founded the Royal Naval Dockyard.

Elizabeth I held a lavish party here to mark her long-awaited accession to the throne in 1558. Then in 1619 King James I had the park encircled with a brick wall. Later still, King Charles II had the park re-landscaped by the French landscape gardener André Le Nôtre (who also beautified St James's Park).

All that and we haven't even got to the bit about the royal Greenwich that stands here *today*.

TEN KING HENRY VIII's ON FILM AND TV

Given that Hollywood stars are encouraged to keep themselves in good shape, there has been a dearth of, ahem, larger actors available to play the King – which has resulted in something of a festival of fat-suits and Tinseltown makeovers. Here are just ten…

Carry On Henry *(1971)*

The Carry On *films are as British an institution as the Royal Family itself. This great British comedy franchise was never going to be reverent, given the subject matter and the* Carry On *reputation for seaside postcard humour. Sid James pads up as Henry but makes no attempt to hide his filthy, cackling laugh, thank goodness. Ludicrously hilarious.*

The Tudors *(TV 2007–2010)*

'Jonathan Rhys Meyers is King Henry 8' – thus ran the advertising copy for the final season of this Canadian-made TV series. Beneath this line, the picture showed a lightly bearded JRM standing arms outstretched, not an ounce of him hanging the wrong way, while the Pussycat Dolls posed in the background behind him… Oh, hang on, those are the six wives in the background, not pop stars. Hmmmm. The New York Times TV reviewer summed the whole thing up perfectly, describing it as a 'steamy period drama… which critics could take or leave but many viewers are eating up.' Ludicrously hilarious in a different way from Carry On Henry.

The Other Boleyn Girl *(2008)*

Features the 'other' King Henry again – slimline and smouldering in the shape of Eric Bana.

The Other Boleyn Girl *(TV 2003)*

The other Other Boleyn Girl *sees Jared Harris – son of Richard Harris – step up to the part in a performance far more in the Keith Michell mould (see below) than the bodice-ripping stuff of recent years.*

Henry VIII *(TV 2003)*

As with Sherlock Holmes, each new generation of TV programme-makers wants to have a tilt at re-telling Henry's tale. Ray Winstone brings heft to the role, both physical presence and charisma.

The Six Wives of Henry VIII *(TV 1970)*

Australian-born Keith Michell fronts a welter of British theatrical talent and brings the King alive for an entire generation of TV viewers in the UK.

The Prince & The Pauper *(1977)*
Big-screen adaptation of the old tale of a poor boy swapping places with a prince sees Charlton Heston keep his shirt on as King Henry VIII.

Elizabeth R *(TV 1971)*
Keith Michell reprises his role, this time in a cameo as Elizabeth's father.

A Man for All Seasons *(1966)*
We remember the great Robert Shaw for his villains (notably in From Russia With Love and The Sting) and for his wild Irish seafarer in Jaws. And he brings an undercurrent of wild villainy to his Henry in Robert Bolt's tale of Sir Thomas More, who refused to recognise Henry as Supreme Head of the Church of England.

The Private Life of Henry VIII *(1933)*
It would take nearly 40 years and the great performance of Keith Michell to unseat Charles Laughton from the throne of King of the Screen Henrys. The movie was the first ever non-American film to be nominated for an Oscar.

The New Greenwich: from King Charles II

Old Royal Naval College, King William Walk, SE10. Tube: Cutty Sark

Changeable types, these royals. Charles II decided that he wanted to replace Placentia with a fashionable new palace in the classical baroque style. So the Gothic terracotta palace was pulled down and replaced by the beginnings of a design by Christopher Wren. But all sorts of financial uncertainty and delays dogged the new palace and the scheme fell into debt. By the time of Charles's death, only the west wing was complete.

James II came next and left the Greenwich project well alone, concerned as he was with the business of the old faith being returned. But with the arrival of William and Mary and the so-called Glorious Revolution of 1688, a revolution of a different kind was wrought on Greenwich.

Out went palaces and in came the Royal Hospital for Seamen **(2)**, as a thank you to all the valiant sailors who had brought Britain to victory at the Battle of the Hague in 1692. Where the land meets the water, the water equivalent of the Royal Hospital at Chelsea (for old soldiers) was born.

The structure that housed this lavish retirement home for those who had served in the British Navy still stands today.

Enter that man Wren again. Sir Chris wanted it to have one big dome as the dominating feature, but Mary still wanted the Queen's House (more of that later) to be seen from the river. So Wren split his big dome into two smaller ones, creating a courtyard in between so that the Queen's House wasn't bullied out of the picture.

The design eventually evolved into four graceful quadrants and the site as it stands today is widely considered to be the finest classical landscape on these islands. Each colonnaded façade mirrors its opposite number in a glory of all things classical baroque. This was Wren's favoured style and, as the term suggests, is a happy marrying of two architectural schools – the classical, typified by graceful columns supporting triangular stone pediments mimicking the temples of ancient Greece; and the exuberant carving of baroque-age swags of fruit and flowers, cherubs and every nautical emblem imaginable, from mermen to the prows of sailing vessels.

Queen Mary died of smallpox in the epidemic of 1694, but a devastated William saw that her wish was carried out and building on the Royal Hospital commenced in 1696.

The naval pensioners arrived in 1705, blue-coated, battle-scarred and keen to get stuck into their beer and 'baccy rations – the great rewards for a life of service. The structure, however, designed as a fitting tribute to the scale of sacrifice made by these embryonic empire-building tars, was simply too grand for its practical use, and was more monument than domicile. The Painted Hall as dining room was particularly ill suited to its purpose.

How's this for a restaurant review, from one Captain Baillie, who, in 1771, complained thus: 'Columns, colonnades and friezes ill accord with bully beef and sour beer mixed with water.'

The pensioners were forced to struggle on in draughty luxury until 1869 when the building became the Royal Naval College. Today it houses the University of Greenwich and the Trinity Laban Conservatoire of Music and Dance.

THE ROYAL FAMILY, THE NAVY AND SEAFARING

King William IV
Nicknamed 'Sailor Bill' thanks to having spent much of his life associated with the navy. Took the throne upon the death of his brother King George IV. Was, at the age of 63, the oldest man to become king of this country... so far.

Prince Philip, the Duke of Edinburgh
Rose to the rank of Commander while serving with the Royal Navy and was mentioned in dispatches in 1941. At the time of writing he is an Admiral of the Fleet.

King George VI
Last royal to see action in the navy – fought in the battle of Jutland in 1916 while still Duke of York.

Prince Andrew, Duke of York
Currently Commodore-in-Chief of the Fleet Air Arm. Saw active service in the Falklands Conflict of 1982. The slight distinction from his grandfather (see above) is that he didn't engage in combat.

Prince Charles, Prince of Wales
Commanded his own ship in 1976 and is, at the time of writing, an Admiral.

King James II
Appointed Lord High Admiral (as Duke of York) after the Restoration.

Queen Elizabeth I
Knighted Sir Francis Drake at nearby Deptford in 1581.

Queen Elizabeth II
Knighted Sir Francis Chichester for his achievement in circumnavigating the globe single-handed. The ceremony took place at Greenwich with the self-same sword used by her namesake some 386 years earlier.

The Painted Hall (3)

Old Royal Naval College, King William Walk, SE10. Open daily 10am–5pm. Admission free. Tube: Cutty Sark

One of the most spectacular dining halls in the world, painted to celebrate British naval supremacy over Europe… the artist also took great care to puff up our only joint ruling monarchs King William III and Queen Mary II. Such is the hagiographic spectacle that just one glance upward at the ceiling will make you say: 'Hang on… I thought we got rid of all that Divine Right of Kings business.'

It is the work of Sir James Thornhill – who was also responsible for the inside of the dome of St Paul's Cathedral (see Chapter 9). It took him 19 years of his life to complete and for his trouble he was paid the not particularly kingly sum of £3 per square yard for the ceiling and £1 per square yard for the walls.

Centre stage in the main ceiling are Peace and Liberty triumphing over tyranny. William and Mary are seated on fluffy clouds in heaven. Apollo shines down on them, as Peace (with her doves and lambs) hands an olive branch to William, who in turn gives the red cap of Liberty to Europe.

Beneath, cast out of heaven, is the defeated enemy Louis XIV, his sword broken (it doesn't take a Freudian genius to read the emasculation metaphor) and wearing yellow, the colour of cowardice and treachery.

No inch of wall was left plain. Whether this was driven by artistic choice or the pound-a-yard business, I'm not sure. Thornhill crammed it with nautical imagery: cannons, anchors, ropes, mermen and mermaids. It's the fine art version of Britannia asking of the waves, 'Who de man?' and the waves replying 'Britannia, you de man, you de man.'

The Queen's House (4)

National Maritime Museum, Romney Road, SE10 9NF. DLR: Cutty Sark; Rail: Maze Hill

How's this for a wedding present: King James I granted his new wife Anne of Denmark the manor and palace at Greenwich in 1613.

Sure beats matching bathrobes.

Anne then employed the one and only Inigo Jones (who had arranged many masques and balls for the Queen) to design her a house truly fit for a queen. The Queen's House still stands today. And it bears all the fingerprints of Jones's experiences on his grand tour of Europe.

Queen Anne was a great patron of the arts and had a passion for architecture and garden design – this last being evident when we gaze upon the Queen's House.

When we throw the word 'revolutionary' about the place, it conjures up images of violent change and upheaval. When we throw it at such an architectural masterpiece as the Queen's House in Greenwich, the modern sensibility shrugs its shoulders and says 'Revolutionary? Huh?'

To the modern eye the symmetry of the building, the pale stone, the columns, the sheer grandeur of the place speak of the established order, the status quo.

Yet in the early 17th Century, such a style was new to these islands. The Queen's House is the first neoclassical building in the country, inspired by the work of the Italian architect Andrea Palladio, after whom we name the Palladian school of architecture.

If that still doesn't seem revolutionary to you, then think of the power of its impact. The style has so captured the British imagination that it remains, for many, the benchmark of architectural taste. Four hundred years down the road, many Britishers still have difficulty seeing beyond the Palladian, the neoclassical. One can see this impact right through our society. Listen to our dear Prince of Wales hold forth on building design, or look at the custom-built modern-with-pseudo-classical-touches pile of any highly paid footballer!

We can only wonder what Queen Anne herself would have thought of such retro tastes, being, as she was, such a dedicated follower of fashion. So much so that it is said she had one of her portraits amended to show her sporting a more up-to-date hairstyle.

Two wonderful and exhilarating views of the Queen's House can be taken in at Greenwich – and I recommend both, each for different reasons.

With the River Thames to your back, the Queen's House is the very picture of symmetry: two rows of seven windows, with a grand curved staircase slap bang in the middle. It is linked to two additional wings by grand colonnades which give the development an air of supreme confidence in its own beauty. It is as if the old place is stretching out its arms and basking in our admiration. The sweeping foreground that leads up to the building is preserved as part of the Grade I listed status of the location.

The second view is more challenging – not least because one has to climb a hill to enjoy it. Looking out from near the Royal Observatory, the backdrop is one of utter modernity with the glass and concrete megaliths of Canary Wharf rising up behind. The Queen's House, however, is far from dwarfed or intimidated by this crowd scene. In fact it looks even grander from this angle, thanks to six columns that grace its upper floor. The view will stir the heart, or boil the blood, depending on one's opinion of modernity in architecture. As with the Albert Memorial (see Chapter 1), no one will simply shrug their shoulders upon taking in this view.

The house was begun on the say-so of Anne, but completed in 1637 by Henrietta Maria, wife of King Charles I. Henrietta had the famous 'tulip stairs' installed – the first centrally unsupported staircase in Britain. It is now part of the National Maritime Museum and plays its part in London's 2012 Olympics as a VIP centre.

Statue of William IV (5)

King William Garden, Greenwich Park, SE10. DLR: Cutty Sark/Greenwich; Rail: Greenwich

As we will see in Trafalgar Square (see Chapter 10), poor old King William IV never did get his equestrian statue.

Perhaps the statue that he did get in Greenwich is more appropriate anyway. There he stands in full naval regalia. He's been here since 1936, having first taken up residence in King William Street in the City of London from 1844. Once a wandering sailor, always a wandering sailor.

From King William IV, the throne goes to Queen Victoria, his niece. Sailor Bill died without legitimate issue. He had ten illegitimate children – all by the same woman. Whether this adds a veneer of respectability to the whole affair, I'll leave you to judge. I'm sure you haven't bought this book as a moral treatise.

The woman in question was Dorothea Jordan, an actress – *quelle surprise* – who enjoyed a 20-year relationship with the King while he was Duke of Clarence. Their children took the name FitzClarence, but the relationship ended when William became king.

As king, William shunned the extravagance of his brother George IV and was known to walk in the streets of London in the early part of his reign. We can count among his descendants through his illegitimate children Mr David Cameron, the Prime Minister who has headed the coalition government from 2010. What would Cromwell say?

A NICE SIT DOWN AND A CUP OF TEA

To the London visitor, Greenwich may seem a little off the beaten track. But as we have seen, a boat trip makes short work of the eastward journey, and when you get there you can graze on the history of, well, the history of everything: land, water and time itself.

Not too shabby a place to eat and drink, either.

On the main drag

National Maritime Museum

Park Row, SE10 9NF. DLR: Cutty Sark; Rail: Maze Hill

The 16° West brasserie lies precisely 16 seconds to the west of the meridian. Who's going to argue about time down Greenwich way? The chefs cook with locally sourced produce where possible and booking is advisable.

The more plainly named Museum Café may sound like the brasserie's frumpy sister, but this is far from the case. The views from the sun terrace are among the best Greenwich has to offer.

Something a little stronger, perhaps?

The Trafalgar Tavern

Park Row, Greenwich SE10 9NW. DLR: Cutty Sark; Rail: Maze Hill

Built in 1837 - the year Queen Victoria took the throne - this riverside pub is one of London's treasures. You'll need to book if you want to eat, but a pint and a sit down for a little read usually isn't too much to ask - although weekends are naturally very busy.

Sssshhh. It's a secret

Goddard's Pies

Fountain Court, off Greenwich Church Street, SE10 9BL. DLR: Cutty Sark

Pie and mash is traditionally the food of the working-class Londoner - and it's almost a London bygone, too, with fewer traditional pie shops remaining open in London with every passing year. Goddard's is still going strong and has been since 1890. A meat pie, with a dollop of mashed potato drenched in a parsley gravy known as 'liquor', is hale and hearty fare. But where to sit when you've bought your food? Is one of London's most beautiful parks, surrounded by 400 years of history, good enough for you?

6 ROYAL EAST LONDON

London's legendary East End polarises the capital's opinion almost as much as the institution of monarchy itself. It is as celebrated in some quarters as it is maligned in others. And legendary is the word. The East has long been the starting point for the peoples of the world as they embark upon their journeys in this, our great capital city. Their experiences of arrival, assimilation, of hardship and victory against the odds are the very stuff of great storytelling.

That their tales have been told and retold aloud makes East London the capital's home of the oral tradition of storytelling. That the tales often have their genesis in the native tongues of the immigrants is important, too. Yiddish elbows its way into English; thieves' argot barges its way in; profane costermonger 'backslang' (a good example of this is 'boy' becoming 'yob') sticks like mud to the everyday talk of Whitechapel. And as the tectonic plates of language shift and collide and merge, a new language is born, the lexicon of the East End.

If the East End is another country with a language all its own, then it will immediately defy governance by the Divine Right of Kings. So surely this means that beyond Aldgate lies a royal wasteland?

Far from it. Dealing as we are with the World's Greatest Soap Opera (with apologies to the Kennedy clan, but I'm afraid you really are *Knots Landing* to our *Dynasty*), the oral tradition can only help heighten the stories, bringing colour (sometimes lurid) and drama (sometimes far-fetched) to the table, along with one other crucial ingredient: sedition.

In the disobedient and unruly East End we can find the roots of British dissent and scepticism alive and well. Not everyone in this country would send them victorious, happy and glorious. As with all truly great tales, there are two sides to the story. And that is nowhere more evident than here in the East End: even where the wildflowers of dissent abound, the patriotic roses still thrive.

And so it follows that it is here in the East End that you will find the Royal Family both more slandered and more exalted than anywhere else in the metropolis. So let's begin with the slander…

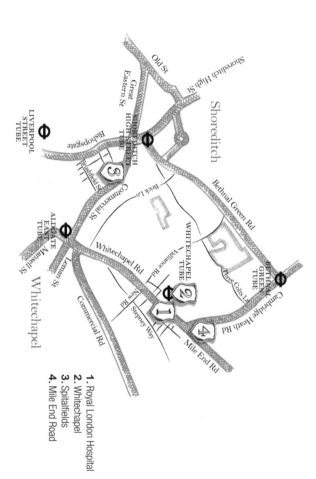

Shoreditch

Old St

Shoreditch High St

Great Eastern St

Bishopsgate

LIVERPOOL STREET TUBE

SHOREDITCH HIGH STREET TUBE

3

Brushfield St

Commercial St

Brick Ln

Bethnal Green Rd

BETHNAL GREEN TUBE

WHITECHAPEL TUBE

Three Colts Ln

Cambridge Heath Rd

BETHNAL GREEN TUBE

ALDGATE EAST TUBE

Mansell St

Lemon St

Whitechapel Rd

Vallance Rd

2

1

New Rd

Stepney Way

CAMBRIDGE HEATH Rd

BETHNAL GREEN TUBE

4

Mile End Rd

Commercial Rd

Whitechapel

1. Royal London Hospital
2. Whitechapel
3. Spitalfields
4. Mile End Road

Whitechapel and Jack the Ripper (1)

Tube/Rail: Whitechapel

It is almost as if that most unfathomoble of all London tales could not survive in the East End if it didn't have a royal element. That character so beloved of the movies – the gentleman killer in white tie and tails and silk hat – is all the more vivid if we have his carriage rattling along The Mall as both the sun and Buckingham Palace recede behind him.

But before we set too dramatic a scene (gas lamps popping into limp life, wan faces lurching at the carriage window for alms, only to be beaten away by the driver's crop and all that business), let's pause to reveal the truth of the tale...

The Duke of Clarence was not Jack the Ripper.

(This 'reveal the end at the beginning' technique never did *Columbo* any harm so we're sticking to it.)

Prince Albert Victor, Duke of Clarence and Avondale – Eddy to his family – was the oldest son of the Prince of Wales (the man who would become King Edward VII) and Princess Alexandra. He is first mentioned in connection with London's most lurid and addictive tale in 1962 – some 74 years after the murders were committed (the case seems to have developed a life of its own with each generation throwing up a new 'suspect').

Broadly, the conspiracy theory runs thus: the Duke of Clarence was a helluva fella for the prostitutes. Some versions have him fathering a child by a prostitute in the East End; others say he married a fallen woman. Queen Victoria, as one might expect, was not amused. The shadowy forces of 'the authorities' kidnap the subject of the Duke's affections and have her lobotomised, thus rendering her mute. The witnesses at the wedding are then hunted down one by one and killed to preserve the good name of the House of Saxe-Coburg and Gotha.

Donald Rumbelow – the great 'Ripperologist' whose prose is refreshingly free of the clammy enthusiasm that so often sticks to the pages of Ripper books – in his definitive *The Complete Jack the Ripper* characterises the Duke as a reluctant soldier, a dandy with a weak constitution, not necessarily the captain of the pub quiz team. This last point alone, that he was not the sharpest tool in the box, gives rise to the counter-theory that he would therefore lack the cunning to wield the sharpest tools in the box.

History has him dead just four years later in the flu pandemic of 1892. Our theory from 1962 has him dead of syphilis – a convenient hook upon which to hang a Ripper conspiracy. Most sources accept that he was shooting in Scotland for at least two of the murders. But our conspiracy theorists rush in here again, saying that he may have been in a psychiatric institution near Sandringham, having been caught in a raid on a gay brothel in Cleveland Street. With Queen Victoria expressing concerns regarding the Duke's 'dissipation' in private letters available to fan the flames, the story shows no sign of going away any time soon.

Spitalfields (2)

Tube: Liverpool Street

Artillery Lane dates from the 1680s, and its name is a fingerprint from the reign of King Henry VIII. The land was used during Henry's reign for military manouevres and training. The Honourable Artillery Company, which claims to be the oldest regiment in the British Army, gained its royal charter in 1537. The location is commemorated with a board detailing Henry's artillery's history on the wall in Sandy's Row, a short, narrow, early Georgian cut-through, the darkness of which is exacerbated by the modern glass buildings that crowd in around as if to conceal its presence out of shame for such an aged street.

The Royal London Hospital (3)

Whitechapel Road, E1 1BB. Tube: Whitechapel

The history of the East End is very much an alternative history of London, the area growing with its proximity to the docks and being shaped by the pollution of the Industrial Revolution borne on the southwesterly wind.

Two London heritage staples stand out by their general absence: blue plaques and statues to the great and the good.

Yet the Royal London Hospital has both.

The London Infirmary from 1740, then the London Hospital from 1748 until 1990, when it became the Royal London, the hospital has strong ties to the Royal Family in the Edwardian era.

Viewing it from the northern side of Whitechapel Road, the side with all the market stalls, the hospital is an imposing edifice indeed. To the western end the landing pad for London's only air ambulance breaks the grim 19th-century lines. Behind the building stands the new wing – a paragon of modernity in blue glass. The overall effect is of a carer in a blue high-visibility vest chaperoning the aged, yet dignified, old lady across the Whitechapel Road.

The other flash of blue is the plaque to the left of the front entrance, dedicated to Edith Cavell, the English war hero of the 1914 to 1918 conflict, who was executed by German firing squad for aiding the escape of British prisoners.

On this building, a plaque could just as easily have been erected to the great children's charity campaigner Dr Thomas Barnardo who worked here (also a Jack the Ripper 'suspect', believe it or not); or to Sir Frederick Treves, the famous surgeon whose base was at the London Hospital.

Treves performed the appendectomy on King Edward VII in 1902 that saved the King's life and allowed him to take the throne on his coronation day in August that year.

The King had stubbornly insisted that, despite the need for an operation, the coronation would go ahead as planned on 26 June 1902. Upon consultation with Treves and the great Joseph Lister, however, the King was informed that the peritonitis (a disease of the abdomen) from which he was suffering would surely take his life without surgical intervention. The coronation was put back, the King's life was saved and almost everyone lived happily ever after. Among those left not so happy were the overseas delegates who had already arrived for the 26 June affair (no small matter of nipping over on easyJet in 1902) and the manufacturers of commemorative china who now had a mountain of dud tea sets on their hands. Edward's coronation went ahead on 9 August 1902.

Treves (born in Dorchester in 1853 and founder of the British Red Cross Society) is also connected to one of the East End's most famous 19th-century tales – that of the Elephant Man.

Joseph Merrick, a native of Leicester and suffering from the condition neurofibromatosis, had washed up on the shores of Whitechapel in 1887 with a travelling freak show that had taken up residence on Whitechapel Road opposite the hospital in a then recently vacated greengrocer's business (at the time of writing it is home to the International Saree Centre). Billed as the Elephant Man – his condition caused extreme growth of excess flesh about the skull and legs, with a stooping curvature of the spine – he was discovered by a curious Treves. Following a circuitous route that took Merrick away to the continent, Treves took him in at the London Hospital.

(Note: Once again, believe it if you will, Merrick is also a 'suspect' in the Jack the Ripper case thanks to his cameo appearance in the 2001 Ripper movie *From Hell*. In fact, to draw a line under the whole Ripper business, it's fairly safe to say that, from this point in the book, whenever you read a famous name, then someone somewhere probably has a theory 'proving' that they were Jack the Ripper.)

Merrick became the subject of a successful Broadway play and David Lynch film (in which Sir Anthony Hopkins played Treves). In his brief lifetime he became something of a cause célèbre, and was even visited by the then Princess of Wales, Alexandra of Denmark.

Princess Alexandra features in the 1980 film version of *The Elephant Man*, played by the English actress Helen Ryan. Ms Ryan had played Alexandra five years earlier in the ITV series *Edward VII* and went on to play Queen Wilhelmina of the Netherlands in the 2002 US TV movie *Bertie and Elizabeth*. Princess Alexandra presented Merrick with a signed photograph which became one of his most prized possessions and it is said that she sent him a card each year at Christmas.

Behind the Royal London Hospital itself, where Merrick resided, that second kind of elusive commemoration can be found: a statue dedicated to Queen Alexandra.

In bronze, the work of George Edward Wade, Alexandra is captured in her coronation robes with the sceptre in her hand. Even taking into consideration that art and artists have long been very kind to our Royal Family, Wade leaves us with the impression of a strikingly handsome woman by anyone's standards. One detail in particular captures the imagination: the hem of her coronation gown is draped casually over the edge of the plinth. It is as if Her Majesty has just clambered back up upon it, perhaps hurriedly so that no one would have noticed her doing so, after performing some good deed here in the East End.

And, indeed, as Princess of Wales, and accompanying her husband, she opened two new buildings at the London Hospital in 1887. But it is for introducing the Finsen light cure for lupus – a disease of the immune system – to England, a fact commemorated on the plinth beneath her, that her statue stands here.

Mile End Road (4)

Tube: Whitechapel/Stepney Green/Mile End

Standing at the junction where Whitechapel Road becomes Mile End Road, with Cambridge Heath Road wending in from the north and Sidney Street raging in from both the south and the bloodied pages of East End folklore (it was the scene of a gun battle and siege in 1911), one can enjoy (or endure) a festival (or riot) of architectural styles.

Making a 360-degree turn, the eye is assailed by anonymous 1980s 'improvements', functional 1950s housing, award-winning 21st-century radicalism and fine examples of 19th-century pubs. It is the perfect spot to indulge in two of the great favourite pastimes of the British: complaining about even the smallest development in architecture since 1840, and banging on about the Second World War.

The war remains a vivid and living London talking point simply because of junctions such as this one – the sheer volume of post-war buildings on view suggests that something must have happened to bring about such wholesale change. The East End, with its proximity to both the business of money in the City and the London Docks, became a prime target at the height of the Blitz.

Enter the woman who would become a legendary, much-eulogised royal figure as the Queen Mother: Queen Elizabeth, consort of King George VI, our wartime monarch.

Legend has it that Queen Elizabeth was once described by Adolf Hitler as 'the most dangerous woman in Europe', given her effects on the morale of Londoners at the height of the savage Luftwaffe attacks by night. Yet the myth of her relationship with the people of the East End did not have an easy birth. To tell the full story we must first undertake the delicate business of dismantling a beloved legend. But by the time we have rearranged the fragments and rebuilt it piece by piece, it will shine even more brilliantly than it ever did before.

HM Queen Elizabeth's first visits to the East End in the early days of the bombing provoked open hostility from those whose lives had been devastated. Dressed in her finery – a decision attributed by some to Elizabeth's view that it would boost morale, to others that it was merely a courtesy to wear one's best clothes when visiting – some accounts have her being heckled and even pelted with rubbish thrown by grief-stricken and rage-addled bomb victims. When Buckingham Palace was bombed – the Royal Family remained 'in residence' but secretly spent their nights 20 miles away at Windsor – Elizabeth uttered one of her most famous lines: 'I'm glad we've been bombed. It makes me feel I can look the East End in the face.'

From this point her East End visits received a heroine's welcome, and the seeds of her populist legend were sown.

Her eternal place in the hearts of Londoners is locked there by the golden key of the following quote, upon being advised to evacuate to Canada with the Princesses Elizabeth and Margaret:

> *'The children won't go without me. I won't leave the King. And the King will never leave.'*

Here at Mile End, some 600 years earlier, royal words formed part of a very different kingly legend. It was at Mile End, on 14 June 1381, that the

14-year-old King Richard II agreed to rebel demands made following the introduction of the Poll Tax, which sparked what we now know as the Peasants' Revolt. The following day he met Wat Tyler, one of the rebel leaders, at Smithfield and confirmed his promise of one day earlier. Wat Tyler was later killed at the scene by the Mayor of London, William Walworth.

And the King soon withdrew his promises of pardon and freedom. Politics was ever thus.

TEN ROYAL PUB NAMES

White Hart: *The White Hart pub that stands where Whitechapel Road meets Mile End Road is named after the emblem of King Richard II and remains a popular pub name all over these islands.*

King's Head: *A tribute to King Charles II, who is held in high esteem by the nation's dipsomaniacs for having the pubs reopened after Cromwell had called time. The Old King's Head on Borough High Street (Tube: London Bridge) is a fine example.*

Royal Oak: *Named after the oak tree in which Charles II concealed himself from the Roundheads during the English Civil War. (Royal Oak, Columbia Road. Rail: Hoxton)*

The Feathers: *The emblem of the Prince of Wales – see also the Three Feathers and, more plainly, the Prince of Wales. (Try The Feathers, just around the corner from St James's Park station.)*

The George: *When not in tribute to one of our six King Georges, then it refers to St George – the cult of whom was brought to these islands by King Richard I. (London's most famous George Inn can be found in Southwark, just off Borough High Street – see the end section in Chapter 2).*

The Duke of York: *A royal title since the 1300s, the Duke of York has become king twice in the past century – George V and George VI. (Try the one at Roger Street, WC1. Tube: Holborn)*

The Blind Beggar: *The blind beggar in question was a heavily disguised Henry de Montfort, who posed as said sightless vagrant to escape Prince Edward (later Edward I) in the aftermath of the second Barons' War in 1263. King John had* been Henry's grandfather. The Blind Beggar pub (Tube: Whitechapel) is integral to the story of the Krays (see our sister volume Bloody London).

Queen of Bohemia: *Eldest daughter of King James I of England and VI of Scotland.*

White Lion: *Emblem of King Edward IV.*

Three Kings: *Usually in recognition of the three wise men, and not the monarchy, with one comic exception: the Three Kings of Clerkenwell (Tube: Farringdon) has a pub sign featuring three kings, one of which is King Henry VIII, the other two being King Kong and Elvis Presley.*

A NICE SIT DOWN AND A CUP OF TEA

In the North, South, East and West chapters, where we cover a wider area of London, the places suggested to stop and have a cup of something reviving and a browse at this book may not necessarily be placed perfectly to strike out to see all the locations in one trip. They will be situated near (or at) at least one of our Royal London sites - and all will provide a warm welcome.

For the purpose at hand, one can approach the East End from two stations - from Liverpool Street (commencing at Spitalfields) or Whitechapel. Decide where you want to rest and relax and choose your station accordingly - there are comfy corners aplenty near both stations.

On the main drag

Andaz Liverpool Street

40 Liverpool Street, EC2M 7QN. Tube: Liverpool Street

Given that our subject matter exists somewhere way beyond posh, we're going to struggle to provide a location in which to imbibe and read that matches the habits of our Royal Family.

But if we can't do truly posh, we can at least go for swish.

Andaz - formerly the Great Eastern Hotel - was designed by the great Charles Barry Jr. Its options range from lounge to cocktail bar. There's even a traditional(ish) pub on the premises, the George. Although be warned: the pub does show football matches on big, plasma screens and can get a bit noisy, especially of an evening. Unfortunately, we can't provide a recommendation for a pub that shows live polo matches (much more in keeping with our subject). Do drop me a line if you know of one.

Something a little stronger, perhaps?

Dirty Dicks

202 Bishopsgate, EC2M 4NR. Tube: Liverpool Street

Famed as being named after the real-life character who inspired Dickens to pen Miss Havisham - Nathaniel (Dick) Bentley's fiancée died before the wedding and he lived a dusty, lonely existence the rest of his days.

The Blind Beggar

337 Whitechapel Road, E1 1BU. Tube: Whitechapel

Fabled East End watering hole associated with 1960s gangsters the Krays. A much more peaceful place these days - and it does have royal associations in its name, as we have seen earlier in this chapter.

Sssshhh. It's a secret

The Market Coffee House, English Restaurant
50/52 Brushfield Street, E1 6AG. Tube: Liverpool Street

There's precious little that's secret about this part of town these days, with the glare of the fashionable spotlight constantly trained eastward. Every conceivable multinational coffee corporation has elbowed its way into the East End this past decade. But it's still possible to sit in a non-homogeneous environment and enjoy great service from a family-run business. They've been here in their current form only since 2001, but parts of the building date back to the 1600s. The interior is composed of the salvaged remains of an old pub. Despite its relative modernity, it achieves a genuinely traditional feel.

Have the cooked breakfast. To hang with your doctor.

INTERREGNUM THREE

Royals around the Monopoly board

The London Monopoly board takes Whitechapel in London's East End as its opening square.

Here's a handy ready-reckoner with which to impress your fellow kitchen-table capitalists when playing the famous board game – one Royal London fact for every square…

- **Old Kent Road:** Kent has been a royal dukedom since 1934 (although it had previously been one in the 18th Century), when it was created thus for the fourth son of King George V. (NB: The Old Kent Road is the road *to* Kent, rather than a road *in* Kent.)
- **Community Chest:** 'It's your birthday. Collect £10 from each player': on the Prince of Wales's 21st birthday, the Queen gave him an Aston Martin.
- **Whitechapel Road:** A statue of King Edward VII can be found opposite the Royal London Hospital.
- **Income Tax:** HM The Queen has paid income tax and capital gains tax since 1992. How much? She's not telling, and neither is HMRC.
- **King's Cross Station:** King's Cross is named after a monument built in the 1830s (now gone) to King George IV.
- **The Angel Islington:** King Henry VIII was fond of hunting in what is now Islington.
- **Chance:** 'Pay school fees of £150': fees for Eton, where Princes William and Harry studied, are around £10,000 a term.
- **Euston Road:** In one of his forays into architectural criticism, Prince Charles once described the Reading Room at the British Library on Euston Road as being like 'the assembly hall of an academy for secret police'.
- **Pentonville Road:** Going back to ancient royalty, the Iceni Queen Boudicca is rumoured to be buried beneath nearby King's Cross station. Rumoured, but not actually true.
- **In Jail:** Queen Mary had her half-sister Elizabeth (I) imprisoned in the Tower of London in 1553.

- **Pall Mall:** In the late 18th Century, the Prince Regent's Carlton House mansion stood on Pall Mall.
- **Electric Company:** Electricity was first installed in Buckingham Palace in 1883.
- **Whitehall:** The last Duke of Cambridge before Prince William can be found in statue form on Whitehall. He lived from 1819 to 1904 and was Commander-in-Chief of the British armed forces.
- **Northumberland Avenue:** Just off Northumberland Avenue, on Craven Passage, stood the Turkish bath where Holmes and Watson once discussed the affair of the Illustrious Client (see Chapter 8).
- **Marylebone Station:** King Henry VIII once had (guess what?) hunting grounds near this spot.
- **Bow Street:** Not the happiest of hunting grounds for royal associations here: Oliver Cromwell moved to Bow Street in 1645.
- **Community Chest:** 'Pay your insurance premium – £20': the Crown Jewels are uninsurable.
- **Marlborough Street:** The timbers of Liberty's store on this street are, in part, taken from HMS *Impregnable*, once the flagship of the Duke of Clarence, later King William IV.
- **Vine Street:** Once the home to the West End Central police station. Since its foundation in 1829, the Metropolitan Police has never had recourse to arrest a member of the Royal Family. Yet.
- **Free Parking:** King Edward VIII is the first monarch for whom we have evidence of an ability to drive.
- **Strand:** Richard II's uncle, John of Gaunt, once lived at Savoy Palace.
- **Fleet Street:** Three queens can be found on Fleet Street in statue form: Victoria, Elizabeth I and Mary, Queen of Scots. The King and Queen pub, alas, is now a sandwich shop.
- **Trafalgar Square:** The Trafalgar Square Christmas tree is presented to the nation by the royal family of Norway. Prince Albert is credited with popularising the Christmas tree in Britain.
- **Fenchurch Street Station:** At the King's Head Tavern that once stood nearby (no. 53, Fenchurch Street), Princess Elizabeth dined upon her release from the Tower of London. On the menu was pork and peas.
- **Leicester Square:** Actors and actresses whose handprints appear in Leicester Square and who have played kings and queens on screen: Sir Ian McKellen has played both Richard II and Edward II, as well as a memorable Richard III; Charlton Heston and Alan Bates both played King Henry VIII;

Dame Anna Neagle played Queen Victoria; Nigel Hawthorne played King George III; Sir John Gielgud played King Henry IV; Sean Connery played King Richard I; Helena Bonham Carter played Queen Elizabeth (the Queen Mother); Colin Firth played King George VI.

- **Coventry Street:** Named after 17th-century Henry Coventry, secretary of state to Charles II, who owned a house nearby.

- **Water Works:** The Diana Memorial Fountain in Hyde Park was the focus of controversy in 2004 when three people were hospitalised from injuries sustained when slipping on the wet surfaces of the 'interactive' commemoration. (For the number of loos in Buckingham Palace, see Chapter 3.)

- **Piccadilly:** The Queen Mother's royal warrant was removed from Hatchard's bookshop, Piccadilly, on her request in 1996 because lurid biographies of Princess Diana were being displayed in the window.

- **Regent Street:** Carreras, the tobacco manufacturer of Regent Street, was granted royal warrants by the Prince of Wales (1866) and King George VI. The latter died of lung cancer.

- **Oxford Street:** Where, in December 2010, Charles's and Camilla's Rolls-Royce encountered around a dozen protestors in the aftermath of an anti-student fees demo. The protestors confronted the car and daubed it in white paint amid isolated cries of 'Off with his head'. Pictures of the incident made the front pages worldwide. The couple were on the way to the London Palladium and were pictured there later that evening seemingly unshaken.

- **Community Chest:** 'It's your birthday. Collect £10 from each player': in this case, the monarch would collect £20, having both a birthday (the day upon which they were actually born) and an 'official' birthday (the day upon which the nation celebrates the event).

- **Bond Street:** The lyricist of 'Rule Britannia', James Thomson, lived above a milliner's shop on Bond Street.

- **Liverpool Street Station:** If you think Liverpool Street station is bedlam today… well it once really was Bedlam – inasmuch as the 'hospital' for the insane once stood on the site. Inmates included would-be assassins of royalty – John Frith and James Hadfield for attempts on the life of King George III and Edward Oxford for the attempted assassination of Queen Victoria.

- **Chance:** 'Drunk in charge. Fine – £20': in March 2007, Prince Harry, a little the worse for wear, lunged at assembled paparazzi when emerging from a night on the Crack Babies at Boujis.

- **Park Lane:** At the top of Park Lane sits Marble Arch, moved to this position from Buckingham Palace in 1851 because reputedly Queen Victoria thought it was ugly.
- **Mayfair:** Queen Elizabeth II was born at 17 Bruton Street, Mayfair.

7 ROYAL WESTMINSTER

Westminster and the Royal Family relationship status: it's complicated.

Westminster is the part of London from which we run the country through our elected representatives in Parliament. Our monarch is a constitutional monarch, acting as head of state within the parameters of elected representation – and has been such ever since King Charles I got himself into such hot water with all that 'Divine Right of Kings' malarkey in the 1640s.

Surely the whole idea is to keep the monarchy at arm's length when it comes to the business of governance. Well, yes… and no.

Like I said, it's complicated.

The current Palace of Westminster dates in the main from 1837 to 1860, the old one having been consumed by fire in 1834. But there has been a palace here at Westminster for nigh on a millennium. Some sources have it that King Cnut (or Canute, the king fabled for commanding the tide to turn back) resided here from 1016. But it was King Edward the Confessor – builder of the Abbey (more of which anon) who established it as the principal royal residence of medieval times. In 1530, King Henry VIII acquired York Palace from Cardinal Wolsey and moved into the building that became…

The Palace of Whitehall (1)

Banqueting House: Whitehall, SW1A 2ER. Tube: Westminster/Embankment/ Charing Cross

Whitehall Palace no longer stands, having burned down in 1698 (dearie me, we have been careless with fire over the years). At its height it was the largest palace in Europe, eclipsing both the Vatican and Versailles.

All that remains of the palace today is the Banqueting House. Built to Inigo Jones's design and costing some £15,000 when it was completed in 1622, it is a pivotal royal building. As we have seen, King Charles I was executed here in 1649, beginning the nation's progress towards constitutional rather than absolute monarchy. And it is also the first completed structure in the neoclassical style, which remains for many the benchmark of tasteful and dignified architectural design.

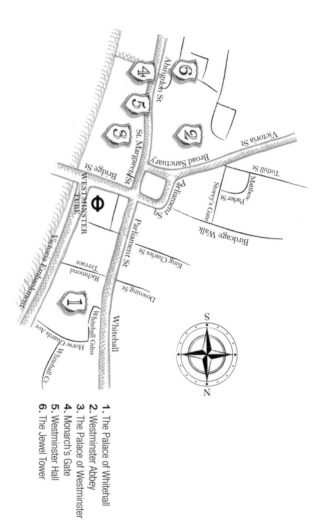

1. The Palace of Whitehall
2. Westminster Abbey
3. The Palace of Westminster
4. Monarch's Gate
5. Westminster Hall
6. The Jewel Tower

The name Whitehall is appended to the street that links Trafalgar Square with Parliament Square and has become a byword for the machinations of government.

On the other side of the site of the old palace, towards the river on Victoria Embankment, a tiny flake of what once was can still be seen. At the eastern end of what is now the Ministry of Defence (the building with the green roof) we can see a number of steps. These are Queen Mary's Steps and mark the spot where the River Thames once met the environs of the palace (the river was famously pushed back, or embanked, from 1862). Beneath this section of the building lies the wine cellar of the Palace of Whitehall with its Tudor brick-vaulted roof.

Westminster Abbey (2)

Dean's Yard, SW1P 3PA. Tube: Westminster

'What's it made of?' is a common walking tour question when approaching many a great London building. And it's an easy one to answer when looking at the Abbey.

What's it made of? Well it's, made of Purbeck marble and Portland stone, to name but two of the building materials.

But it's held together by whopping great dollops of English history.

Founded in 1042 by pious monarch Edward the Confessor; Ted the C hoped that his building would please God and he'd thus be guaranteed a place in heaven. No mere dropping an extra coin in the plate and helping old ladies across the road for him.

He had the Abbey built in the Norman style with sturdy, squat columns and rounded arches – there's a depiction of the original in the Bayeux Tapestry, a very different building to the one we see today.

When Edward died he was canonised and his shrine was placed in the centre of the church – the only English king to be sainted. And so the tradition of royal burials began at the Abbey. And within two years, following the victory of William, Duke of Normandy in 1066, the great tradition of coronations began, with King William I elbowing his way to centre stage on Christmas Day.

In 1245 (just in time for lunch? no, I mean the year), King Henry III – dubbed the Builder King, thanks to his appetite for construction – decided to start again. This is more or less the early English Gothic Abbey as we see it today. Influenced by some of the French cathedrals he had seen, King Hank wanted a more opulent church for coronations and royal burials.

The two 'bookends' of the Abbey were added later: at the far eastern end (the Parliament end) the King Henry VII chapel was added on his request between 1503 and 1511; and at the western end the two towers were added by Christopher Wren's successor as the Abbey's surveyor, Nicholas Hawksmoor to give the Abbey a more impressive silhouette on approach. This is the twin-towered, picture-postcard view that is conjured up at the very mention of England's foremost church.

Westminster Abbey is a royal peculiar– that is to say, a place of worship that comes under the personal jurisdiction of the monarch. It is the only royal peculiar outside the walls of a royal residence, all others are within the grounds of a palace. The other London royal peculiars are: the Chapel Royal and the Queen's Chapel at St James's Palace; the Chapel Royal at Hampton Court; and the Chapel of St John's and the Chapel of St Peter ad Vincula at the Tower of London.

WEDDINGS

Starting with the most recent… did you watch The Wedding? What do you mean which wedding? *The* Wedding: 29 April 2011, the marriage of Prince William and Catherine Middleton, of course.

Great, wasn't it. Horse-drawn carriages, red-uniformed soldiers, crowds of well-wishers, TV crews, statesmen, celebs and the entire British Establishment on display.*

Well, get this: that was *not* a state occasion. That was a private wedding. Albeit a very big one.

The Abbey has been the venue for 16 'royal weddings' to date – a figure that includes two of Queen Elizabeth's four children – Princess Anne (to Captain Mark Phillips, 1973) and Prince Andrew (to Sarah Ferguson, 1986) – as well as the Queen herself (to Prince Philip in 1947).

Prince Albert, Duke of York, was married to Lady Elizabeth Bowes-Lyon in 1923 at the Abbey. And it was at this ceremony that a great tradition was born.

(*Missing dignitaries included our most recent prime ministers Gordon Brown and Tony Blair, while Sir John Major, Blair's predecessor, was in attendance. 'Sir' here is the key and neither Blair nor Brown have yet been knighted. The wedding being a private affair, there was no protocol for either their inclusion or exclusion. Sarah Ferguson, Duchess of York, was also missing. Popular speculation has suggested that she is persona non grata in royal circles given her involvement in a cash-for-access scandal in 2010, although such tales are seldom if ever confirmed officially by St James's Palace. Rumours that the Duchess may have been smuggled into the wedding under her daughter's voluminous fascinator remain unconfirmed.)

A delay in the proceedings was caused when Winston Churchill arrived late. In the ensuing hiatus, the bride laid her bouquet on the Tomb of the Unknown Warrior.

From the wedding of King Richard II to Anne of Bohemia in 1382, to that of minor Hanoverian Princess Patricia of Connaught to the Honourable Alexander Ramsay in 1919, not a single flake of confetti fell on the hallowed stones of the Abbey. That the most famous church in England went without a royal wedding for half a millennium seems odd to the modern observer.

But from 1923, when Prince Albert (later King George VI) married Elizabeth Bowes-Lyon, the old place seems to have hardly had a rest between nuptials.

TEN WILLIAM AND CATHERINE WEDDING BITS

- *A global audience of 2.5 billion watched the wedding.*
- *1,000,0000 well-wishers lined the route for Wills and Kate (as we are no longer allowed to call 'em, of course. It just wouldn't do to have a Queen Kate. It would be like having a King Darren. Just not on).*
- *That dress (#1)... The Royal School of Needlework at Hampton Court Palace had no idea they were embroidering the wedding gown. They were thrilled when they recognised their handiwork on the famous dress designed by Sarah Burton at Alexander McQueen.*
- *That dress (#2)... The seamstresses had to wash their hands every 30 minutes and the needles were renewed every three hours to keep the lace clean and delicate.*
- *That dress (#3)... The lace motifs included a rose, a thistle, a daffodil and a shamrock to represent England, Scotland, Wales and Northern Ireland.*
- *William's uniform was cut by Gieves & Hawkes of Savile Row.*
- *Full-grown trees were used as wedding flora at the Abbey for the first time – field maples and hornbeams wheeled into the Abbey with great difficulty. Cost was high –in the region of £50,000 – but they were very environmentally friendly as they have been replanted.*
- *The American bank Merrill Lynch donated £1 million to help spruce up the Abbey – a process which included a restoration of the 14th-century coronation portrait of King Richard II, who had also been married at the Abbey.*
- *If you type any of the following phrases into Google – 'cartwheeling vicar', 'cartwheeling priest', 'cartwheeling verger' – you will find a number of sites with footage of a Westminster Abbey official cartwheeling for joy down the aisle of England's most famous church. Before he does so, he looks around to see if anyone is looking. When he ascertains that he is not being watched, he spins into action, forgetting all about the still-rolling TV cameras.*

> ■ *The surge in demand for electricity at the end of the wedding, caused by an estimated 1 million kettles being switched on, was a third higher than that recorded after Charles and Di's wedding in 1981 – but Charles and Di did have a million more well-wishers than their son lining the route. So we'll call it a draw.*

FUNERALS

QUEEN ELIZABETH, THE QUEEN MOTHER

As with weddings, we'll begin with the most recent first, that of Queen Elizabeth, the Queen Mother in 2002. By her own request, her funeral wreath was placed upon the Tomb of the Unknown Warrior in an echo of her now famous wedding day gesture 79 years earlier. Her final resting place is St George's Chapel, Windsor, by her late husband and her younger daughter Princess Margaret.

DIANA, PRINCESS OF WALES

As a tour guide with London Walks, I have spent much of the early 21st Century answering visitors' questions about the events of 6 September 1997 – the public funeral of Diana, Princess of Wales.

Were there really that many people? Yes, plus 2 billion worldwide on TV.

Were there as many flowers as they say? Yes, a metre-and-a-half deep at Kensington Palace, many of them transferred to Parliament Square.

Did the whole nation go into mourning? Yes, I believe it truly did, one way or another. Even for the most staunch republican, the outpouring of grief was difficult to avoid.

Did it reach hysterical proportions? No, I don't believe so: the shock, the suddenness of it all served as some kind of anaesthetic, with the most extreme feeling of the period being a kind of surreality.

But these are merely my impressions of the time. Others would have different memories: confusion, perhaps, at the perceived emotional distance of the Queen from the national mood; rage on the radio phone-ins.

The esteem in which Diana was held is, of course, central to the national reaction, summed up so succinctly in Tony Blair's speech at the time (see Chapter 8).

That Prince Charles remained a bachelor for so long is also a factor. Thirty-three years old is no great age to surrender to nuptial bliss these days, but when one is the heir to the throne, it is inevitable that speculation on such matters becomes almost a national sport. The perceived length of time that Charles held onto his single status created a great wave of royalist euphoria – or even relief – in 1981 for a people starved of royal spectacle for a generation. (The Prince's investiture as Prince of Wales in 1969 was nice and all that, but archaic ceremonies are not what made Disney rich.)

We Britons who have lived through the past 175 or so years have lived through a period of comparative royal calm: two long-reigning monarchs, Victoria and Elizabeth, have accounted for around 120 years of this period. Okay, we've had abdication and three divorces to keep us amused in recent decades. But it's a mere bagatelle compared with even just the reign of King Henry VIII, or of any of the other royal legends on which we Brits are fed with our mother's milk.

Thus entire generations had come and gone without witnessing the machinery of state swing majestically into action on big royal days. Such a day was the wedding of Diana and Charles.

And such a day was 6 September 1997.

Eight Welsh Guards accompanied the coffin. The Duke of Edinburgh, Prince Charles, Prince William, Prince Harry and the Earl Spencer joined at St James's Palace.

King Juan Carlos of Spain, Princess Margriet of the Netherlands and Constantine II of Greece were in attendance at the Abbey. Nelson Mandela was there. Prime Minister Tony Blair read from the First Letter to the Corinthians: 'And now abideth faith, hope, love, these three; but the greatest of these is love.' Figures from the world of show business included Elton John, who sang his 'Candle in the Wind' (with lyrics rewritten by Bernie Taupin). Earl Spencer's eulogy had strong words for both the Royal Family (the Earl stated clearly that he respected 'the tradition' into which Diana's sons had been born) and the press, claiming that she was 'the most hunted person of the modern age'.

OTHER ROYAL FUNERALS

Following the funeral of King George II in 1760 there was not another funeral of a monarch or consort in the Abbey until 1925, when Queen Alexandra left the stage.

ROYAL BURIALS

The Abbey is also known as the resting place of the famous: poets, painters, politicians, musicians, scientists and statesmen – the cluster burials as they are sometimes known. But the original intention was that the Abbey would be a royal mausoleum – and it is.

There are 17 monarchs (not including spouses) buried in the Abbey. When we include wives and consorts, the body count rises to two dozen. We'll look at the most interesting internments below.

The tradition of royal burials changed because of King George III's preference for Windsor (you have to be mad to prefer anywhere over London – and, lo and behold, he was, thus proving my point). He – and George and William iV, Victoria, Ted Seven and Georges V & VI – are all interred at St George's Chapel, Windsor.

QUEEN ELIZABETH I AND QUEEN MARY I

Good Queen Bess is buried alongside her half-sister Bloody Mary. Do you think someone is trying to tell us what to think of them: Good and Bloody?

Although both are buried in the same tomb, it is only Elizabeth's effigy that can be seen carved in white marble. Both queens struggled with religious unrest and dealt with their own beliefs in very different ways, but in reference to this there is a memorial stone laid in 1977 remembering those divided or martyred in the name of Catholicism or Protestantism. Even in death, our royals get themselves into a bit of a narrative tangle. Families, eh?

MARY, QUEEN OF SCOTS

Directly opposite on the south side of the Abbey, a similar chapel contains the tomb of Mary, Queen of Scots.

Whoa there. What's she doing here?

Again: it's complicated.

There she is, lying under the same roof as her cousin Elizabeth, who signed the death warrant for her execution.

And Mary's tomb is much more lavish than Elizabeth's. Her fine effigy lies beneath an elaborate canopy covered in thistles and at her feet sits the red lion of Scotland, wearing a crown and almost roaring in victory.

How did such a thing come to pass?

When Elizabeth died childless in 1603, the next in line to the throne was Mary's son, James VI of Scotland. When 'Jamie the Saxt of Scotland' then added the title King James I of England to his CV, he had his dear old mum's body moved to the royal church and buried in a tomb fit for a queen.

INNOCENTS' CORNER

Two miniature tombs contain King James I's baby daughters, who died in infancy, and on the wall is a stone casket that holds the bones of the two little princes, 15th-century Edward V and his brother Richard (see Chapter 9).

MEMORIALS

In Poets' Corner (see the section on poets laureate, page 57) a memorial to Laurence Olivier can be found. Ennobled to the level of the Right Honourable the Lord Olivier as Baron Olivier of Brighton in 1970, and wearer of a number of Shakespearean crowns, Olivier's great contribution to our royal tale is his voice-over for the film of the coronation in 1953, *A Queen is Crowned*. (Olivier himself was no stranger to coronations and blue blood, having played Kings Richard III and Henry V on screen, as well as the Prince of Denmark, Hamlet.)

CORONATIONS

The business of crowning our monarchs is central to the story of Westminster Abbey and has been since that French fellow William of Normandy came a-conquering in 1066.

The coronation itself remains a lavish and highly theatrical ceremony. Given our love of pomp and circumstance was it ever going to be anything else? Did you think it was just a small matter of lobbing a bling-encrusted hat on some-one's head and then all off to the after-party? No no no.

During the proceedings the new monarch undergoes six stages of symbolic ritual to elevate them into the tradition.

CORONATION: A STEP-BY-STEP GUIDE
Does it all seem a bit theatrical, this coronation business?

To be fair, it's an aspect of the day that we are not unaware of.

When King Henry III had the Abbey rebuilt, he had the coronation specifically in mind. A raised dais can be found at the heart of the building in an area known as – what else? – the theatre.

Stage by stage (no pun intended), here's how we go about crowning a monarch (this is your cut-out-and-keep guide for that most paradoxical of things: a great day that we hope is a long, long way off. Like I said, it's complicated)...

Stage one: recognition
The new monarch enters the Abbey and there is a procession (ooh, we love a procession) down the nave to the theatre. There are peers (folks from the House of Lords) in red robes and there is much saluting and shouting of 'Vivat!' (the Latin for 'Long live!')

(When you think of the whole thing as being not unlike the last reel of Star Wars, *then it doesn't seem so weird or frightening.)*

Stage two: oath
There's always serious stuff wrapped up in our pageantry. The monarch must now swear to govern the populace by the laws of the land and act as Defender of the Faith.

Stage three: consecration
The monarch is then escorted to the coronation chair – a gold-painted wooden chair installed by King Edward I. After his seizure of the Stone of Scone in 1296, Edward I had a special shelf made to hold it – symbolic of his suppression of the Scots (the Stone of Scone was the ancient Stone of Destiny on which every Scottish king had been crowned since time immemorial).

At this point we must pause to borrow, appropriately, from Sir Walter Scott... It is now, gentle reader, that we take to a seemingly leafy literary glade away from the beaten path of our narrative to deal with the Stone of Scone.

Brought to the Abbey as above, the King issued the instruction to bring 'that turd' as a trophy. Although some say that the monks at Scone Abbey had already cast the real one to the bottom of the River Tay upon hearing Edward's army approach. Some others say that, when the Stone was stolen/liberated on Christmas Day 1950 by four Scottish students, then the thieves/liberators returned a copy and not the original to Westminster. I once met a man in Oban who said his Uncle Jimmy had the real one in his back garden. But then I met another chap in Fife who said he had it in the cupboard under his stairs.

Once the monarch is seated, the consecration is performed where the sovereign is anointed and baptised using holy oil administered by the Archbishop of Canterbury to the backs of the hands, the breast and the forehead.

Stage four: investiture
The dressing up bit. The monarch is dressed in the coronation robes and ornaments – the outward symbols of inward and spiritual grace.

This fabulous costume change, transforming someone who is just really, really, really posh into an actual ruler, begins with the aptly named supertunica (originally modeled on a Roman consul's dress uniform), followed by the imperial mantle, which is heavily embroidered with shamrocks, fleurs de lys, roses and thistles.

Both garments are made out of woven gold thread and combined weigh 23 pounds (10kg).

Next the sceptres. The sceptre with the cross symbolises temporal power under the cross; the sceptre with the dove, equity and mercy.

Once all the regalia has been presented, the actual crowning can take place. Did you think I'd forgotten about the crown?

St Edward's Crown (named after Edward the Confessor, founder of the Abbey) is placed on the sovereign's head and then all present shout 'God Save the queen/ king' – deleting, of course, as appropriate.

Stage five: enthronement
The penultimate stage in which the monarch is physically lifted from the coronation chair to the throne. When one becomes king/queen, one no longer has to worry about walking short distances between the furniture.
Once enthroned the homage can begin…

Stage six: homage
The peers and peeresses in attendance now don their coronets and caps and process to bow and pay homage to the new monarch.

Finally, holy communion is then taken and the new sovereign withdraws to St Edward's Chapel for the last costume change into purple velvet robes and the more familiar Imperial State Crown (the one the Queen wears on the stamps) for the procession out.

Phew. How to follow that? Only Samuel Pepys could even try.

After Charles II's coronation in 1661, Pepys, impressed and overawed, wrote: 'I may now shut my eyes against any other objects… being sure never to see the like again in this world.'

Quite so, Sam.

Queen Elizabeth II was crowned at the Abbey on 2 June 1953. It took Abbey staff six months to prepare for the occasion and 3,000 guests crammed into the Abbey on the day.

The BBC set up their (at that point) biggest ever outside broadcast to provide live coverage of the event on radio and television (the broadcast was made in 44 languages). Sales of television sets boomed – the embryonic medium was given a great fillip on the day we acquired our Prince Philip.

An estimated 3 million people lined the streets of London to watch the royal procession.

In that post-war age of shortages and rationing, there was an insufficient number of professional coachmen to transport dignitaries to the Abbey and so businessmen and country squires offered their services on the day, dressed up as Buckingham Palace servants.

The great Trinidadian calypso singer Young Tiger (born plain ol' George Browne) recorded the events of the day on his 78rpm record '(I Was There) At the Coronation'. In the lyrics of the song, he described the royal couple thus:

> Her Majesty looked really divine
> In her crimson robe furred with ermine
> The Duke of Edinburgh, dignified and neat
> Sat beside her as Admiral of the Fleet.

(You can hear Young Tiger and all the other great calypsonians of the Windrush generation on the wonderful album *London is the Place for Me* on Honest Jon's Records.)

TEN CORONATION TREATS

William I
When William I was crowned on Christmas Day, the language barrier posed a few problems. When the subjugated English guests shouted their consent during the recognition of the new king, the French Norman soldiers though they were protesting and in retaliation began burning local houses, thus causing chaos and confusion and a general exodus from the Abbey.

Richard II
Richard II was only 11 years old when he was crowned and fell asleep half way through the ceremony. To be fair, it is a long day for a kid. His recently restored coronation picture hangs on one of the left-hand columns of the nave.

George I
Again, language was the problem – this time the German–English divide. When George I was crowned, he understood nothing as he did not speak a word of English so his coronation was exceptionally long-winded with translators on board. He remained resolutely oblivious to the language of his peoples throughout his reign.

George IV

Money. Marital strife. An embarrassing scene. Big hair. Is it a scene from Dynasty? If not, it can only be King George IV. Never one to go in for understatement, he had the most expensive coronation ever, spending £24,000 on his robes alone – the cost did include a gigantic wig which proved a little too warm during the ceremony as his thick makeup began to melt and drip.

George IV (#2)

His estranged wife Caroline of Brunswick could be heard outside the Abbey hammering on the West Door and shouting to be admitted... but to no avail. George had ordered that his detested spouse should be locked out and she eventually gave up and went home.

George IV (#3)

George related after his coronation that both the Bishop of Bath and Wells and the Bishop of Durham were so nervous that neither could find the oath. And so the King had to read it from the Archbishop's book (the order of service) and then, to top it all, when St Edward's Crown was placed on the King's head, it was back to front.

Queen Victoria

At Queen Victoria's coronation the royal jewellers Garrard and Co. made the coronation ring too small and the Archbishop had to use considerable effort to force it onto her fourth finger. Victoria later recorded in her journal: 'I had great difficulty to take it off again – which I at last did with great pain.' At least they had 64 years to get the next one right.

King Henry VI

Longest wait for a coronation: seven years. King Henry VI was only months old when he became the king in 1422. He was crowned in 1429.

Edward V, Lady Jane Grey, King Edward VIII

Ted V and LJG were both deposed before they were crowned. Edward VIII abdicated after just 326 days. In the case of King Edward VIII, his coronation arrangements carried on regardless – all that changed was the head upon which the crown was placed, that of his brother George VI on the self-same day in May 1937.

Queen Elizabeth II

A minor hiccup, really, in the scheme of things. It rained. Typical.

The Palace of Westminster (3)

Edward the Confessor was so pleased with the result of building a Benedictine monastery – or minster – west of the old city that he had a palace built next door. Building began in the late 1040s.

Shortly afterwards William the Conqueror chose it as his main home and so it became the main residence of the kings of England for the next 400 years, until the reign of King Henry VIII when Whitehall, Hampton Court and Greenwich became his favourites. But although it went out of fashion as a royal residence, it continued to be the centre for the administration and practical running of the country, functions that still take place on the site of the old palace today.

It was not the palace of fairytales with points and pinnacles and graceful symmetry but a bit of a medieval mishmash, a chaotic and ever-spreading collection of half-timbered buildings arranged around a series of courtyards. The majority of buildings were made of wood – stone was expensive and time-consuming to use – but there were two notable exceptions: Westminster Hall and the Jewel Tower.

Today, the Jewel Tower and Westminster Hall are all that is left of the former royal palace and residence; the old palace burned down in the fire of 1834 and today the new Palace of Westminster stands on its site, the seat of government in the UK.

At the western side of today's Palace of Westminster, our bicameral Houses of Parliament, we find a statue of Oliver Cromwell. The spectre at the feast, the elephant in the room, we had to get around to him sooner or later.

Cromwell came first in the English Civil War, had the king beheaded, and took over the running of the country with no monarch as Lord Protector of the Commonwealth. His statue serves as a reminder that we have a constitutional monarchy and not an absolute monarchy.

The statue caused controversy in the 1890s when the Irish Nationalist Party protested about the public funding of the statue, Cromwell providing rare common ground for Irish republicans and traditional British monarchists. (Cromwell's army and their brutal treatment of the Irish people in the 1640s sees Cromwell invoked as a figure of hatred for many in Ireland to this day.)

The statue was privately funded by Lord Rosebery. Legend has it that the Irish MPs only agreed to the statue because it would be situated in 'the well' outside Westminster Hall and would therefore be almost hidden – the statue's proponents had failed to reveal the size of the plinth that boosts ol' laughing boy to impressive prominence. Such chicanery in the Mother of All Parliaments? Surely some mistake…

Upon the restoration of the monarchy, Cromwell's severed head was displayed on a spike at Westminster Hall (the building before which he now stands) following his posthumous 'execution' in 1661.

(We've been rather over-fond of such gruesome punishments in our island story down through the centuries, and I'd just like to point out here that we do nice things in England, too: we drink tea, we play cricket, we grow roses.)

Westminster Hall is the oldest remaining part of the old Palace of Westminster still standing within the parameters of the new palace (we'll deal with the adjacent Jewel Tower later).

Houses of Parliament

Westminster, SW1A 0AA. Tube: Westminster

The Palace of Westminster, our Houses of Parliament, remains a symbol of both London and Britishness the world over – particularly the clock tower, or Big Ben as it is popularly known. The palace takes centre stage in the royal story at...

THE STATE OPENING OF PARLIAMENT

The State Opening of Parliament is where the worlds of pageantry and the serious business of governing a modern country collide – in a fireworks display of ritual and ceremony.

As a major state occasion, security is naturally very high. Debate on our high surveillance society will have to wait for another book – you may have noticed, er, one or two CCTV cameras on your travels through our great capital. But security has long been an issue here at Parliament and the first 'tradition' that is observed on the day of the State Opening of Parliament is the Yeomen of the Guard making a precautionary sweep of the cellars. The spirit of ol' Guido Fawkes and his Gunpowder Plot of 1605 still looms large over the whole affair.

The next tradition that is observed is the ceremonial hostage taking of an MP.

(Of all our ceremonies, this is the one where we go right over the top.)

Before the monarch leaves the palace to go to Westminster, a Member of Parliament is taken to the palace to act as a hostage in the event of Parliament turning ugly (or even uglier than usual) in the presence of HRH. (It's that man again, King Charles I, who back in 1642 stormed into Parliament and demanded the arrest of five members for treason. He was given short shrift and, quite against the spirit of forgive and forget, no monarch has been allowed into the House of Commons since that time.)

Bear in mind that all this happens before the monarch has even set foot in the Roller. This is just the prelude.

Next up is the crown, travelling in its own state coach. Yes, HM's hat travels in style even when on its own. At Victoria Tower* (the square tower at the opposite end of Parliament to Big Ben), the crown is passed by the Queen's Bargemaster** to the Comptroller of the Lord Chamberlain's office. Along with the Great Sword of State and the Cap of Maintenance, the crown is carried to the Royal Gallery.

The monarch enters by the Monarch's Gate **(4)** – a gilt-edged, wroughtiron gate at the base of Victoria Tower where he or she is received by the most senior members of the House of Lords. These Lords then accompany the monarch into the Robing Room – yup, they've got a special room set aside for this – where the Imperial State Crown (see Chapter 9) and robes are donned while other members of the House of Lords congregate in traditional ceremonial gowns. (In the modern era, many Lords are gowned in fake ermine, to show their opposition to hunting for fashion purposes.)

A fanfare of trumpets sounds – which is good news because that almost always means that we're getting a procession. Sure enough, the monarch and attendants then process through the Lords to the throne where the monarch is seated. Enter Black Rod.

He has the best part.

Bearing in mind that the sovereign is not welcome in the House of Commons, he/she has to knock at the door. But he/she is the king/queen, and ain't gonna knock on nobody's door, no how, no way.

So the sovereign has a chap to do this on the royal behalf.

Black Rod – for 'tis surely he – is dispatched to tell the Commons to get their sorry behinds out of the chamber and into the royal presence.

The door of the Commons is duly slammed in Black Rod's face to symbolise the Commons' independence since the days of the Commonwealth.

(*Victoria Tower is the entrance to the House of Lords – remember that the monarch is barred from the House of Commons.)
(**The Queen's Bargemaster is a post that seldom crops up down the Jobcentre. Today it is a largely ceremonial post, with the Bargemaster being in charge of the 24 Royal Watermen, each of whom are salaried at £3.50 per annum.)

Black Rod – a Knight of the Most Noble Order of the Garter (see Chapter 9) – then summons the members of the House of Commons by banging on the door with his big (black) stick (rod). Three times. Loudly.

It is a great and deeply theatrical moment.

The door of the Commons chamber then opens – reluctantly – and then the MPs follow him, talking loudly to symbolise their independent voice to the House of Lords.

The Lord Chancellor then presents the gracious speech to the monarch to read. HRH has no hand in the writing of the speech – it is composed by the government and outlines their policies and what they hope to achieve over the parliamentary session.

The ceremony usually takes place around November and, although we can't attend unless we are taking part, it still affords a great opportunity to get a glimpse of the monarch on duty around Westminster on the day.

Westminster Hall (5)

Westminster, SW1A 0AA. Tube: Westminster

Westminster Hall was built between 1097 and 1099 and was originally used as a magnificent banqueting hall. It was the largest banqueting hall in Europe and was the marvel of all who visited. William II had great plans for augmenting the palace – all cut short when he was killed in the New Forest in 1100.

Later, Richard II beautified and improved the hall by employing architect Henry Yevele (who completed the Abbey's nave around the same time) to design a new porch and roof, elevating the height of the hall by half a metre. The King's motif – the white hart – was incorporated into the décor and, perhaps most impressively, an oak hammerbeam roof was installed – the work of Hugh Herland. It remains the widest unsupported span in the country.

The hall soon became used as an administrative centre. Grand Councils and early Parliaments were held here and from the 13th Century to the late 19th Century it was most famously used as a law court.

The hall has on occasion been used for royal lyings-in-state – Edward VII and the Queen Mother – as well as for that of Winston Churchill in 1965.

The Jewel Tower (6)

Abingdon Street, SW1P 3JX. Tube: Westminster

Built at the same time as Westminster Hall got a new roof, and again credited to Henry Yevele, the Jewel Tower was built between 1365 and 1366 of Kentish ragstone specifically to keep not only the Crown Jewels but also other valuable royal possessions safe: solid gold dinner services used for banquets, fur-trimmed robes and other fine pieces of schmutter, damask, gold cloth and heavily embroidered tabards.

Three storeys high and surrounded by a moat, it was a very successful treasure house and was used as such until Tudor times, when King Henry VII had the Crown Jewels moved to the Tower of London and the fine livery to the King's Wardrobe in the city.

From 1621 to 1864, parliamentary records were kept here; then, from 1864 to 1938, it was used as a weights and measures office. Today it is a fascinating museum run by English Heritage detailing the architecture and development of the old Palace of Westminster.

A NICE SIT DOWN AND A CUP OF TEA

If one wanted to read this chapter inside an actual palace, the best thing to do would be to write to your MP and apply for a guided tour as one of his/her constituents. You'd have to keep your fingers crossed that the MP in question was amenable enough to end the tour with a nice cup of tea and a sit down in the Commons canteen. And if it all pans out, then at least you'd have something to read rather than having to listen to a politician droning on.

Not very practical, all told.

Luckily, local alternatives abound.

On the main drag

Methodist Central Hall
Westminster, SW1H 9NH. Tube: Westminster

Unwilling as I am to quote verbatim from publicity materials, the website of Methodist Central Hall has this little nugget with which it is very difficult to take umbrage. It describes 'an excellent cafeteria in the basement where visitors can enjoy light refreshments, mid-day meals and teas'.

Quite so. As a busy place of worship, and as a conference centre, Methodist Central Hall has reduced access from time to time, but when open it provides a lovely little oasis in the heart of raging Westminster. Check opening times on their website at www.methodist-central-hall.org.uk.

Something a little stronger, perhaps?

Walkers of Whitehall
15 Craig's Court, SW1A 2DD. Tube: Charing Cross

It's not often that converted banks, churches and former municipal buildings make good pubs - they often make large pubs, but that's not necessarily a good thing.

Walkers is the exception.

Formerly an Irish bank, it is tucked away behind the busier pubs of Whitehall and does a rather nice bite to eat, too - baguettes, sharing platters. And a drinks menu that caters to wine drinkers as seriously as it panders to beer aficionados.

Sssshhh. It's a secret

~~Westminster Cathedral~~
42 Francis Street, SW1P 1QW. Tube: Victoria/St James's Park

Seems odd to be talking of secrets in plain view of the heart of Europe's biggest city, but the café in the crypt at Westminster Cathedral may just qualify for such an epithet. No mention is made of it on the cathedral's main website, and there are no signs outside the building itself.

Perhaps a little odd, too, to suggest a Roman Catholic church for a book on the Defenders of the Faith - but, as we have seen, the Protestant faith is only some 500 years old in our tale. Almost half of our story is set against the backdrop of the Old Faith; the other half is told in spite of it. Where better to read it than England's principal Catholic church.

(Tip: when you've had a read and a cup of tea, the gift shop provides access to a lift which will take you to the top of the tower to enjoy one of the best views in London. The ride costs £5 and the view is priceless.)

8 ROYAL WEST LONDON

The first thing we do in Royal West London is remove Kensington from centre stage and give her a chapter all to herself. In this manner, we will not be upstaged by the glamour of Diana, the legend of Victoria and the clamour of modern-day royals at play.

Despite taking both Diana and Victoria out of the story – much like Shakespeare resting his lead characters, in Act Four – we are left with the very stuff of royal storytelling. In places it's as if a producer has thrown the script back at the writer, demanding 'Gimme castles! Gimme palaces! Gore! Romance!'

Brentford

Rail: Brentford

Famed among 1970s TV watchers as the home of Brentford Nylons, and to football fans as the home of Brentford FC, whose ground (my husband assures me) has a pub at every corner, the largely peaceable nature of this West London suburban town belies a history of royal strife.

The Battle of Brentford may not be as famous a name to Britons as the battles of Britain or Waterloo. But Brentford can outdo both in terms of numbers of battles named in its honour, given that the Battle of Brentford features in not just one but two episodes of royal history.

The location that is now Syon Park saw some action in the Battle of Brentford and is currently the location of a Hilton hotel and a garden centre. The garden centre – the first of its kind – was opened by HM Queen Elizabeth II in 1968 and is dotted about with plaques reminding us of the site's ancient and royal heritage – a pleasant spot to sit indeed, a blend of old (tea and scones in the café) and new (free wi-fi). But the royal history of this manor is a far, far bloodier affair...

The first Battle of Brentford took place in 1016 between Cnut and Edmund Ironside (Edmund II). Edmund, defending lands inherited from his father Ethelred the Unready, was victorious at Brentford but went on to lose the war and his lands were shared between him and Cnut. The precise date of the battle is unknown but it is believed to have taken place between May and October of 1016. And who was the goody and who was the baddy? Depends. If Brad Pitt

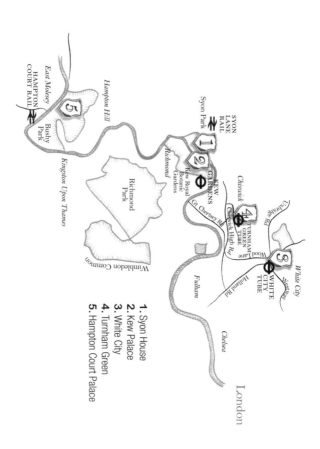

1. Syon House
2. Kew Palace
3. White City
4. Turnham Green
5. Hampton Court Palace

London

ever signs up for the movie, then, depending on the spin of the producer, he will play handsome, lantern-jawed Edmund who defends his lands from marauding invaders, or handsome, lantern-jawed Cnut taking what is rightfully his from the greedy English king (Hollywood loves an English villain). Either way, he will get the girl.

The Battle of Brentford II, to use the Hollywood sequel numbering system, forms an important scene in the seismic drama of the English Civil War. It took place on 12 November 1642 and is described by many sources as a 'small' pitched battle. Small, perhaps, to an historian armed with a pen fighting only a deadline, but pretty sizeable if you ended up in the debit column of the day's statistics: an estimated 170 dead.

The Royalist cavalry was commanded by Prince Rupert of the Rhine – is it the alliteration of his name and title that sends chivalric shivers up the spine? – the 23-year-old nephew of King Charles I. In portraits (including one by Anthony van Dyck), the Prince, with his pout, his pallor and his flowing locks, comes over like the sensitive bass player from some prog rock band from the early 1970s. In battle, however, he was not so fey.

At Brentford, the Royalists won the day, but were delayed sufficiently by the Parliamentarians to derail their bid to take London. And without London, the war could not be won.

Syon House (1)

Syon Park, TW7 6AZ. Rail: Syon Lane

Were one to ask of a young child 'Draw me a castle', the result would not be a million miles away from the building that now stands in Syon Park.

The crenellated home of the Duke and Duchess of Northumberland has an appropriately fortified look given that its history, and the history of the site, has been touched by some of the more dramatic episodes in our royal history.

Syon Abbey (named after Mount Zion in the Holy Lands) stood here until the reign of King Henry VIII and the dissolution of the monasteries. It had been a favourite retreat of Catherine of Aragon. It was also where Katherine Howard was confined just before her execution in 1542. In 1547 King Henry VIII's body rested here on its way to Windsor for burial. Legend has it that the coffin burst open in the night and that the dogs of Syon House had at his not inconsiderable remains – a tale told as divine punishment following Henry's laying waste to the abbey.

John Dudley, the Duke of Northumberland, was the father-in-law of Lady Jane Grey and it was at Syon House that she began her nine-day reign as queen.

Syon House then reverted to Queen Mary, who, in 1557, encouraged the nuns to re-establish the abbey, but her sudden death in 1558 saw the ascension of Queen Elizabeth I and the plan was aborted. In 1594, Henry Percy, the 9th Earl of Northumberland, took up residence through marriage into the Devereux family – the house has been the London residence of the Duke of Northumberland ever since.

A happy ending? Dear me, no. The story of the Royal Family, which has no qualms about lurching from historical biopic to action thriller in the blink of an eye, is seldom far away from a violently dramatic set piece. In 1605, Henry Percy's Roman Catholic cousin Thomas Percy swung by for a bite to eat before heading off to hook up with one Guy Fawkes and his plotters in their ill-starred attempt to blow up King James in the Gunpowder Plot.

Although Northumberland was in no way involved in such seditious activity, it didn't look good, breaking bread with a terrorist and all that. Northumberland spent the next 15 years as a 'guest' at the Tower of London for his trouble.

A later Duke of Northumberland commissioned Robert Adam to redesign the interior in the late 18th Century – indeed, Northumberland was one of Adam's principal patrons. In the same period, Lancelot 'Capability' Brown redesigned the gardens.

The film *Gosford Park* was shot in part at Syon House.

Kew Palace (2)

Royal Botanic Gardens, Kew, TW9 3AB. Open April–September. Tube: Kew Gardens; Rail: Kew Bridge

The Royal Family have always travelled in style: from the Queen's Flight to the royal train, from the vintage Rolls-Royce that made us all go 'ooh, nice car' even when it was pictured on Oxford Street being assailed by violent protesters, to the Prince of Wales's Aston Martin flashing out of Buck Pal driven by a dashing Duke and with his comely new bride by his side, romance has never really left the world of monarchic travel. Perhaps it is this detail that is the most obvious divide between royal and commoner in the more egalitarian modern era: the commoner is herded aboard budget planes and crammed onto far-from-budget trains; the royal is not.

It was ever thus: the royals have long known that the best way to cut through London is on the water. Our east–west waterway is an underused thoroughfare in the 21st Century. King Henry VIII, say, could flash between his birthplace at

Greenwich and his happy hunting grounds out Richmond way in double-quick time – with, perhaps, the added advantage that he didn't have to run into the likes of you and me travelling by road.

There has been a palace on the banks of the Thames at Kew for almost 400 years. Queen Elizabeth I gave the original palace to her great favourite (ahem) Robert Dudley. In a rebuilt version, Frederick, Prince of Wales (son of George II, father of George III) resided there.

The author Max Hastings, in a *Daily Telegraph* article, wrote an endearing piece on dog-inspired poetry in which he related a tale of the poet Alexander Pope gifting a dog to Frederick with an inscription on its collar that read:

I am His Highness' dog at Kew.
Pray tell me, sir, whose dog are you?

This second palace dated from 1631 and was in turn replaced by a structure of which King George III himself had a hand in the design. Gothic in style, it was not a well-loved building and was torn down during the reign of George IV with its fixtures and fittings distributed through other royal palaces – most famously, its staircase being redeployed at Buckingham Palace.

Today's Kew Palace, the fourth, stands opposite the site of the previous palace and was once a manor house known as the Dutch House.

Kew is one of those palaces that confounds the expectations of the first-time visitor – particularly those from the great republics of the world where palaces are few and far between if they exist at all.

Let's begin with the building material, for it is in the chasm between the physical matter of the structure and the image conjured in the mind's eye by the word 'palace' that we find the seeds of potential disappointment.

Whenever the word 'palace' comes into play, the imagination rightly begins to assemble a range of opulent materials with which to work. And indeed the imagination should never be fettered by budgetary constraints.

When one approaches a palace made of brick, such as Kew, the romantic heart sags with a quite natural disappointment. Brick only enters the realm of the fairytale as a high-security precaution against windy wolves. We must also hold Hollywood to account – and not just because it is something of a British national sport to do so – because the early years cinema experiences of children the world over are littered with towers and turrets and marble and gold.

Keep in mind also that it has been the case since pretty much the 1660s that when the Royal Family want to build a palace, then the budget has to be agreed by those in real power – the parliamentarians.

All this is merely to bring expectation down to something approaching a normal level – and when we achieve this, then the palaces in question can recapture their ability to astound and delight. (A similar approach can also be applied a little to the east at Kensington.)

Here at Kew, as with Syon House, we have a palace that strikes a chord in another part of the childhood imagination, away from Disney turrets.

The symmetry of Kew Palace almost suggests that at any moment its bright terracotta-coloured façade will split perfectly in two, swing open, and the world's most majestic doll's house will be revealed. Its manifold and irregular chimneys add a childlike dimension to the design that delights utterly.

In 2006 the Prince of Wales hosted a dinner here to celebrate the Queen's 80th birthday. Soon after, the palace opened to the public after a 10-year hiatus due to restoration. Drapes and soft furnishings using period techniques of manufacture were added and new disabled access brought the building into the 21st Century.

If you are visiting Kew and want to have a nose around inside, make sure to plan your visit in the summer months – the palace is closed in winter as it is unheated. Its exterior is a delight all year round.

White City (3)

Tube: White City

Both the first and the most recent of the three London Olympics can be found on the Central Line – Stratford in the east for 2012, and White City in the west for 1908. But as the new buildings that gleam in the east have just been finished for the 2012 games, the 1908 games are now so distant as to be almost Grecian in the memory.

Yet in its day the White City stadium was considered a modern marvel. Built for the Franco-British exhibition of 1908, most of the Olympic events of that year were held here, in an era when one arena would suffice for the whole festival.

Our Royal Family are seldom far from the sporting life of the nation. Queen Alexandra was in attendance for the Olympic marathon. Indeed, it had been her suggestion for the finish line to be repositioned close to the royal box, rather than at the gates of White City stadium, so that she could have a better view of the climax of the day. This suggestion followed her previous request for the starting line to be moved back into the grounds of Windsor Castle rather than at the gate, so that the royal children could witness the starting gun.

What answer other than 'Yes, Ma'am' could the Olympic organisers give to the Queen?

Which is all well and good – unless you are Dorando Pietri, the Italian runner who attacked the race at full pelt in that most rare of conditions – a hot, sunny day in London. By the time he entered the stadium, not only were his knees of jelly, but his mind seemed to be of custard, addled by the heat and his own punishing pace, and he turned the wrong way. The race marshals shooed him in the right direction like some errant chicken rebelling the coop, at which point he collapsed. Dragging himself to his feet, he made a last Herculean effort to cross the line, but collapsed again.

Good old British decency cannot stand idly by in such circumstances. With Pietri down, a couple of chaps in straw boaters stepped forward to help the poor fellow over the finish line… at which point the Italian was disqualified for cheating.

It has long been speculated that Pietri would have taken gold had the start and finish line remained in the original places, with the race a mere 25 miles long (as it had been since the 1896 games in Athens). The marathon distance of 26 miles 385 yards, as set by Queen Alexandra's bespoke requirements, remains the one used to this day.

An epitaph to this tale leads to one of the great myths of the day – that Sir Arthur Conan Doyle was one of the chaps who helped the stricken runner cross the line. Not quite true. Conan Doyle, in conjunction with the Queen, had a hand in creating a special trophy for Pietri, who had won the hearts of the British people with his stout-heartedness. But the creator of Sherlock Holmes did not come physically to the aid of Pietri in his moment of need. The myth springs from Doyle's role in the special trophy and the fact that one of the chaps in the famous photograph of the event wears a moustache almost as impressive as that of the great writer's own.

Conan Doyle went on to write of Queen Alexandra's husband, King Edward VII, albeit in a most oblique way. 'The Adventure of the Illustrious Client' features a client so illustrious that his name is never once mentioned. We assume it to be the King himself.

RAF Northolt

Ruislip, HA4 6NG. Tube: Ruislip Gardens

RAF Northolt is the home of the Royal Flight and is the reason why the paps (tabloid slang for paparazzi) are seldom able to stick their long lenses up the noses of the major Windsors. (The minor Windsors, of course, are deemed to be fair game at Boujis, see Chapter 1.)

This functional backdrop took centre stage in the immediate aftermath of the events of 31 August 1997 – the death of Diana, Princess of Wales. Her body arrived here having been flown from Villacoublay Air Base, Paris. Among those in attendance were the Station Commander of RAF Northolt and the RAF Chaplain-in-Chief, as well as Prime Minister Tony Blair, fresh that day from minting the phrase 'the People's Princess'.

It was initially believed that his chief spin-doctor Alastair Campbell had invented the phrase, but Campbell later went on to credit Blair himself with the creation of the title that passed into the language. Some have suggested that the Windsors resented the appellation, as it canonised Diana while immediately demonising her former in-laws, and that it forced the Royal Family, including Diana's sons, to return to London from Balmoral and grieve in an all-too-public arena. Others are of the mind that it saved the Royal Family from a terminal PR disaster in making them return to London.

The events of 31 August saw the establishment of a 'new tradition' in the Royal Family. Many people were unhappy that the Union Flag did not fly at half-mast over Buckingham Palace to mark Diana's death. Protocol at the time was this: when HM The Queen was not in residence, the Royal Standard did not fly. The point being this: the Royal Standard can never be flown at half-mast – there is always a monarch. The Queen is dead, long live the King.

In the aftermath of this monumental event in British royal history, a new protocol was introduced. When the monarch is away from home, the Union Flag will fly in the stead of the Royal Standard. Thus, if an event deemed to be sufficiently important to the nation takes place, then the Union Flag can be flown at half-mast. Such a practice was observed on the death of Queen Elizabeth, the Queen Mother in 2002.

TEN LANDMARKS IN DIANA'S FUNERAL LONDON

Diana, Princess of Wales had many connections with London through her life; her death and its aftermath also left indelible fingerprints on the landscape of the capital.

RAF Northolt
Scene of her return to Britain (see above).

Kensington Palace
Floral tributes 1.5 metres deep surrounded the palace gates. Tributes continue to be left here – although in decreasing numbers – on the anniversaries of her birth and death.

Westminster Abbey
Funeral service in the presence of 2,000 mourners with an estimated 2 billion following worldwide on TV.

St James's Palace
The oldest inhabited royal palace in London – location of Diana's lying-in-state five days prior to the funeral.

Hyde Park
From where mourners watched the funeral service on big screens. Location of the Diana Memorial Fountain, opened by Queen Elizabeth II.

Funeral route
The route was reported thus by the BBC in 1997:

> 'After the service, the hearse will journey from the Abbey to Constitution Hill. From there it will proceed slowly to the M1 along streets expected to be lined by hundreds of thousands of mourners. From Constitution Hill, the cortege will continue to Apsley Way and Wellington Arch. It will then proceed to Hyde Park Corner and along Park Lane, Cumberland Gate, Tyburn Way, Marble Arch, Oxford Street, Portman Street to Gloucester Place. Turning towards Lord's cricket ground, the procession will swing along Park Road to Wellington Road (A41) and then north along the busy Finchley Road. Moving into Hendon Way, it will then journey over the Brent Cross flyover, where thousands more will turn out to pay their respects. The cortege will negotiate the streets of North London on its way to the family home. It will then proceed around the North Circular Road (A406) to Staples Corner.'

Royal Courts of Justice
Scene of the 2007 inquest into the death of Diana and Dodi Fayed which returned the verdict of death by grossly negligent driving by the chauffeur Henri Paul and the attendant paparazzi.

> **Harrods**
> Site of a memorial (lower ground floor, at the far end of the Egyptian Hall) to both Diana and Dodi Fayed, erected by then-owner of Harrods Mohamed Al-Fayed.
>
> **Walk**
> A seven-mile route marked by 90 plaques taking in four royal parks: St James's Park, Green Park, Hyde Park and Kensington Gardens.
>
> **Playground**
> The Diana Memorial Playground in Kensington Gardens is regarded by many to be the most appropriate memorial to the late princess. Taking J.M. Barrie's Never Never Land as its theme, there is a pirate ship, tepees and lost boys' hideouts.

Turnham Green (4)

Tube: Turnham Green/Chiswick Park

It's a leap of imagination today, from the blameless suburban outposts of the District Line to a pivotal moment in the English Civil War. Yet Turnham Green provides us with just such an opportunity.

The Battle of Turnham Green saw a vastly outnumbered Royalist force under King Charles I turn away from engaging with the raggle-taggle army of the Parliamentarians who, although superior in numbers, were made up of inexperienced men.

The location of the battle can be seen at today's Acton Green and Chiswick Common, most of which has been built over.

Hampton Court Palace (5)

East Molesey, KT8 9AU. Open daily throughout the year. See www.hrp.org.uk/HamptonCourtPalace for opening times. Rail: Hampton Court

The whole point of palaces such as Hampton Court was to provide a retreat from the hubbub of the city for the king or queen. Hampton Court remains just such a rural idyll, resting on the banks of the Thames just outside the boundary of London. But such is its proximity in the modern era (30 minuntes by train from Waterloo) that no royal-watcher should miss a trip to Henry VIII's old stamping ground.

HENRY VIII

Word association time. What images are conjured up by the mention of King Henry VIII? Multiple wives? Of course. A beard? Yes. Beheadings? Well, only a couple to be fair, but yes we associate him with execution.

Anything else?

Are we tiptoeing a little bit around the subject here? Dare we mention… girth? Heft? (Although, as we have seen in Chapter 5, he wasn't always old and fat, and once looked like Jonathan Rhys Meyers!)

I'll leave it to the words of one of my walkers on a London Walks Tower of London tour. As I turned to lead the group to the next treasure, I overheard a mother give her five-year-old an explanatory footnote to my commentary:

> *'You remember Henry VIII, darling. He was the big fat king.'*

Quite so.

This abiding image is thanks in part to the great kitchens at Hampton Court Palace.

Henry denied himself nothing and one of his great passions was for food – a moment on the lips, 500 years on the hips, it would seem.

His love of feasting is reflected in the sheer size of the Hampton Court Palace kitchens. Today restored to meticulous 16th-century realism, the kitchens – mission control for Henry's appetite –are perhaps the most vivid of this great palace's exhibits. Their prominence and volume bring to life the sheer excess of Henry's court.

They are formed of three enormous multipurpose Tudor kitchens plus a whole courtyard with rooms specialising in different food preparations – pastry kitchens, boiling house, buttery, butchery, bakery, spicery, as well as flesh and fish larders.

A master cook was employed to create banquets – the Gordon Ramsay of the whole affair – with a dozen other cooks assisting. Don't forget the mob-handed supporting cast of kitchen hands, pantry boys and turnspits.

As to the menu, peacock was considered to be the ultimate treat. The bird, once dead, would be very carefully skinned so that its feathers remained intact. The body of the bird would then be roasted and, when cooked, would be popped back into the skin so that it looked as lifelike as possible. It would then make a spectacular centrepiece to a banquet table. Swans could also spend their life looking forward to such a fate.

Hampton Court Palace became Henry's showpiece palace, a reflection of his tremendous power and wealth. No lowly accolade this, considering he had 60 royal residences to choose from by the time of his death in 1547.

Hampton Court has come to encapsulate Henry's reign and life – even through it was originally built for someone else: Cardinal Thomas Wolsey.

In the early years of Henry's reign, Wolsey had been the power behind the throne of England. When Henry became king he was a young and attractive playboy and was much more interested in having fun – good-looking and athletic, he loved dancing and making music as well as huntin', fishin' and shootin'. Showing little interest in running the country, his most senior minister, the Lord Chancellor – Thomas Wolsey – was the man in charge.

Ambitious, from a lowly background (his father was an Ipswich farmer), Wolsey had chosen the church as a path to the top. Intelligent and ruthless, he rose through the ranks of bishop and archbishop, becoming a religious adviser to Henry VII. When Henry died, Henry VIII promoted his father's right-hand man to the position of Lord Chancellor.

Wolsey became wealthy. Too wealthy. And he lacked discretion in how he splashed his cash. In 1514 he bought the land for Hampton Court with a wonderful view of the river. He also enclosed 1,800 acres of land around the palace, today Hampton Court Park and Bushy Park.

Building began in earnest. Made of eye-catching red brick and terracotta, the palace emerged like some gorgeous cake, ornamented with turrets, heraldic beasts and barley-sugar twisted chimney pots as well as extensive grounds and gardens.

On completion it contained 1,000 rooms and was ample enough to accommodate 280 guests in luxury. It was also the first palace with proper bathrooms with piped water – revolutionary stuff.

The interior decoration was second to none, with fabulous wooden panelling – intricate carving known as linenfold panelling because of its resemblance to carefully folded linen sheets. The floors were covered in priceless carpets, the walls adorned with tapestries woven from gold and silver thread, and there were cabinets containing gold and silver plate worth £2 million – it was without a doubt the finest palace in England.

Many of those original features can still be seen in the palace today.

The cherry on Wolsey's ample cake came with his elevation to cardinal at the behest of the Pope in 1515.

But Henry was a jealous and suspicious man (we missed those famous attributes when we made our earlier checklist). The King grew jealous of Wolsey's wealth and suspicious of his power, and in 1525 things began to turn sour for the cardinal.

After a weekend visit to the palace, Henry turned to Wolsey and asked: 'Why does a man of God need a palace such as this?'

Wolsey, realising he was out of favour, answered: 'So that I might make a present of it to my King.'

Which was the correct answer.

Having got his hands on Hampton Court, Henry made it bigger (surprise surprise) and grander still, adding a tennis court, a tiltyard and a new banqueting hall and augmenting the aforementioned kitchens.

Five out of six wives who expressed a preference opted to live at Hampton Court Palace – Anne of Cleves was the exception. Jane Seymour gave birth to Henry's only son, Edward, in a bedchamber here – but she died just three days after he was born. Katherine Howard was arrested here and the Haunted Gallery is said to be where her spectre runs screaming as the king's soldiers pursue her before capturing her and taking her to the Tower.

Catherine Parr, his last wife, married Henry here at the Chapel Royal – the Tudor fan-vaulted ceiling of which was installed in 1535 and made of solid oak from Windsor forest. She is said to have exclaimed when Henry proposed marriage: 'Sire! It was safer to be your mistress than your wife.'

But, for once, King Henry VIII is only half the story.

Hampton Court is really two palaces for the price of one.

WILLIAM AND MARY

When husband and wife makeover team King William and Queen Mary first visited the palace, they fell in love with its situation – location location location. But in their usual bulldozing style (see Chapter 5) they decided the stuffy old Tudor palace really would have to go and a more fashionable Wrenaissance building should replace it.

Enter that man again, Christopher Wren, who was all too keen to pull down the Tudor palace. Luckily for us, he commenced work on building the new palace first, and never got around to swinging the wrecking ball.

What is left behind today is the most delicious architectural coup de théâtre: one enters under the gatehouse of a Tudor palace and emerges into the gardens via a classical façade. Time travel made easy.

The work from this period is what led to Hampton Court being described as the Versailles of England.

Because William and Mary were ruling equally as dual monarchs, not one but two sets of state apartments were needed – the Queen's apartments and the King's apartments.

It was one of William and Mary's favourite residences because it was situated in the health-giving countryside. Both were keen garden lovers and created beautiful ornamental gardens in the Dutch style. Today, the privy garden has been restored to look exactly as it did in 1702 – in the style known as parterre, where the grass is cut into shapes and different-coloured gravels are used to create symmetrical patterns. The garden was designed to be viewed from the first floor of the palace.

Subsequent monarchs were well disposed towards Hampton Court. George II kept his two ugly-sister-like mistresses here: one perceived to be (ahem) a larger lady, the other tall and scrawny. Their nicknames were the Elephant and the Maypole.

When Victoria came to the throne she opened up parts of the palace and its famous maze (created in the early 1700s by Queen Anne) to the general public.

A NICE SIT DOWN AND A CUP OF TEA

Our West London sites are so spread out that the three pit stops we're going to recommend are each at specific royal sites. With some of our other chapters - East London for example, and even Westminster - the sights can be taken in on one single visit if you are pushed for time. Here in West London, the royal sites are so rich that a day is insufficient time to drink everything in - Hampton Court itself is a day's pleasure at least!

Hampton Court Palace
East Molesey, KT8 9AU. Rail: Hampton Court

If you get the weather, then the obvious thing to do is picnic here. The 60-acre gardens, beautifully landscaped and with views of the Thames, provide a veritable smorgasbord of perfect spots. The fountains and horse-drawn tram provide a gentle soundtrack. A nice cup of tea (or coffee) can be had at the Privy Garden Coffee Shop.

Kew Palace
Royal Botanic Gardens, Kew, TW9 3AB. Tube: Kew Gardens; Rail: Kew Bridge

The Kew Orangery, while not particularly successful in the business of growing oranges (which were moved to Kensington in 1841), was once the largest glasshouse in England. A soup and sandwich offer at £6 is a popular option, but if a cuppa and a cake are the order of the day, there's also the Victoria Gate Café.

Please note that the Orangery and Victoria Gate Café are part of Kew Gardens, and can only be accessed if you have bought a ticket for the Gardens. The Orangery can be contacted on 020 8332 5680.

Syon House
Syon Park, TW7 6AZ. Rail: Syon Lane

Syon House is open from March to October, Wednesdays, Thursdays, Sundays and Bank Holiday Mondays, 11am to 5pm (last entry 4pm). In winter the gardens are open at week-ends, but the surrounding park is accessible the year round and forms part of the Capital Ring orbital walking route. The Refectory at Syon Park is open daily for snacks, drinks and light lunches - their number is 020 8568 0134.

INTERREGNUM FOUR
Ten portrayals of members of the Royal Family in fiction and alternative histories

- ■ 'The Adventure of the Illustrious Client' Published in 1924, the client's identity in this Sherlock Halmes story is a matter of some secrecy but is almost certainly King Edward VII.

- ■ 'Rodney Stone' The Prince Regent makes a cameo appearance (as do Lord Nelson and Beau Brummell) in this non-Sherlockian Arthur Conan Doyle tale from 1896.

- ■ *To Play the King* Michael Dobbs' novel is part of the political House of Cards trilogy of thrillers. It achieved notoriety when transferred to the screen for the BBC with scenes that suggested that the nocturnal habits of the King (widely considered to be loosely based on Prince Charles) included paying for, er, 'dating'.

- ■ *SS-GB* Len Deighton's dramatic alternative history sees King George VI a prisoner in the Tower of London in Nazi-occupied Britain.

- ■ *The Leader* Guy Walters, in his 2003 alternative history, explores the much-discussed Nazi sympathies of King Edward VIII. His narrative restores the King to the throne with Wallis Simpson as queen and Oswald Mosley as dictator/prime minister.

- ■ *Fatherland* Edward VIII is again back in charge – as Emperor of the British Empire – with Princess Elizabeth in exile in Canada in Robert Harris's acclaimed alternative history thriller set at the time of Hitler's 75th birthday celebrations.

- ■ *The Other Boleyn Girl* Fascinating fiction by Philippa Gregory based on the 'forgotten' tale of Anne Boleyn's sister Mary. Published in 2002.

- ■ *Flashman and the Tiger* George MacDonald Fraser's hilarious prig Flashman (a character extrapolated from the bully in *Tom Brown's Schooldays*) claims in this the 11th Flashman novel not only to be familiar with the Prince of Wales (later King Edward VII) but also to have been familiar – in an entirely different way – with Edward's mistresses Lillie Langtry and Daisy Brooke.

- *Twenty Years After* Alexandre Dumas's novel features the execution of King Charles I at Whitehall.
- *Jonathan Strange and Mr Norrell* Susanna Clarke's acclaimed fantasy/alternative history novel from 2004 features King George III.

9 THE TOWER OF LONDON AND THE CITY

The Tower of London (1)

Tower Hill, EC3N 4AB. Open daily throughout the year. See www.hrp.org.uk/TowerOfLondon for opening times and prices. Tube: Tower Hill

'What tower? I can see a castle. But I don't see no tower.'

Not an uncommon response, this, from visitors with whom I spend time on walking tours. The ravages of time have had little visible effect on the might of the Tower of London either physically or on its place in English history. But time – and the appearance of the BT Tower, Tower 42, the Gherkin and their like – have seen our dear Tower of London seem, well, not so Tower-like in recent centuries. It's a case for the Trade Descriptions Act.

What we have to do here is put ourselves in the rudimentary turnshoes of your average subjugated Anglo-Saxon circa 1090. You'd been rubbing along quite nicely thanks, under King 'Arold until that nasty business at' Astings with the harrow – sorry, I mean arrow. You're harbouring a grudge. William the Bastard (as was his nickname) has taken over your land. You want revenge. You start to formulate a plan… and then you look up and see the Tower of London.

At 90 feet tall it may not dominate the 21st-century skyline. But in the 1090s, our dispossessed and ill-shod ancestors would have looked at the imposing edifice on the waterfront with a gulp. 'Them Normans,' we would have said to ourselves, 'they mean business. They're serious people.'

(Perhaps they needed such a statement of authority given that those Norman haircuts, if the Bayeux Tapestry is to be believed, were snigger-worthy in the extreme.)

The complex that stands by the water today has spread and developed considerably since the 11th Century and is, these days, assailed only by armies of visitors – some 2.5 million of them in 2010. They come in search of a flake or two of English history – and they leave with bucketfuls of the stuff.

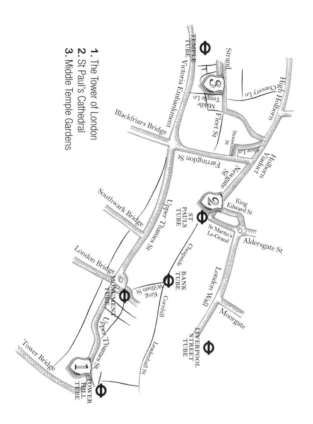

1. The Tower of London
2. St Paul's Cathedral
3. Middle Temple Gardens

Beheadings, imprisonments, defence of our island realm, the Royal Family's past, the Royal Family's present, an ongoing love of pageantry (red uniforms abound) and folklore (the ravens) – the history of the entire nation is embodied in the building commonly just known as simply the Tower.

Substance really does win out over size at this World Heritage Site.

Schoolchildren – and Blue Badge guides! – are taught the basic facts of the Tower in much the same way as budding musicians learn where the notes belong on a musical stave: with a mnemonic – E(very) G(ood) B(oy) D(eserves) F(avour).

Over at the Tower, there's a musical flavour too when we employ MOZART as our reminder of the purposes for which the old place has been used: M for museum, O for observatory, Z for zoo, A for armoury, R for royal residence and T for torture. There was a certain inevitability about that last one, wasn't there? Our monarchs have seldom been big on forgiving and forgetting.

The museum aspect is plain to see today – the visitors throng the place to see the Tower's most famous 'exhibit'… the Crown Jewels.

The Crown Jewels

As is always the case with our dear Royal Family, nothing is really very straight-forward. There's more to the Crown Jewels than just a fancy hat and a bit of bling. Far more.

The Crown Jewels as a term covers the glittering regalia worn by the monarch and members of the Royal Family on high days and holidays.

Described as the nation's collection of priceless treasure, these items include crowns encrusted with diamonds, rubies, emeralds and pearls, as well as symbolic pieces of kit used during the coronation ceremony.

Also included are solid gold dinner services and cutlery used for state banquets and fine centrepieces designed to impress the guests and dignitaries invited to royal feasts.

Much of the regalia dates from the 17th Century and the reign of Charles II. As we have seen elsewhere in this book, England became a de facto republic after the Civil War (although we mostly shy away from the 'R' word).

Lord Protector Oliver Cromwell, however, was as much a fan of the violently symbolic gesture as the regime that he had overthrown. Amidst his raft of draconian You're-Not-Here-To-Enjoy-Yourself policies, he went methodically about the business of destroying the trappings of monarchy. The Crown Jewels were high on the list of stuff for the chop (ahem), symbolising as they did to Cromwell the 'detestable rule of kings'.

Immediately after King Charles I's execution, the Lord Protector ordered that the Crown Jewels 'be totally broken'. His parliamentary commissioners carried out his orders with alacrity and gusto. Much of the gold was melted down, precious gems sold off and sceptres cut in half – a nice bit of Freudian symbolism this, although you'd be a brave soul to suggest such a thing to Cromwell in person.

This all becomes a problem in 1660 upon the restoration of the monarchy and the need for a coronation, at which point King Charles II throws up his hands and utters the age-old cry of the belle of the ball: 'O! But what shall I wear?'

Fortunately there were precise records kept of the old regalia and so a list of new ornaments required for Charles II's coronation was drawn up and executed (careful with that word when Cromwell's around) by Sir Robert Viner, the royal goldsmith. The new set of Crown Jewels cost just over £12,000 – closer to £18 million in today's terms.

And it's more or less those new ones (they're only 400 years old) that we can see at the Tower today.

THE IMPERIAL STATE CROWN

The bit most of us think of when we talk of the Crown Jewels. It is worn at the State Opening of Parliament. If you're reading this far away from the Tower but still want to see it, then it's the one that Her Maj is wearing on our postage stamps. And very fetching it (and she) looks too.

If you haven't got access to a stamp, you could try making your own crown at home. It's really very simple...

Recipe for an Imperial State Crown

Ingredients:

- One gold crown
- Velvet
- Ermine
- 2,868 diamonds
- 1 sapphire from the ring of St Edward the Confessor
- 1 sapphire from the crown of Scots King Alexander II
- 15 ordinary sapphires

- 11 emeralds
- 4 large drop pearls
- 273 smaller pearls
- 1 Black Prince's ruby
- 4 ordinary rubies

Method:

- Fashion your crown with four crosses pattées (the crosses with arms narrow in the middle that grow wider at the ends) around the sides.
- Pop another cross pattée on top.
- Alternate your crosses pattées with four fleurs de lys.
- Line your crown with the velvet and ermine.
- Encrust it with the diamonds and other ordinary gemstones.
- Set the sapphire from the ring of St Edward the Confessor in the uppermost cross.
- Set the other sapphire – the one you have acquired by vanquishing Scotland in 1290 – in the band of the crown.
- Above this sapphire set the Black Prince's ruby – a gift of Don Pedro the Cruel of Castille, the one worn by King Henry V at the Battle of Agincourt.
- Attach the drop pearls – preferably ones that have once belonged to Mary, Queen of Scots and have been acquired as macabre souvenirs of her beheading – to the bottom of the topmost cross.
- Allow the glue to set.
- Browse some internet comparison websites for a good insurance provider.
- Shop around for a case with shatterproof glass at least two inches thick. Invest in every conceivable security innovation known to man. Invest in research into every possible security innovation currently unknown to man. Employ the British Army to guard it.

Simple.

THE TOWER OF LONDON AND THE CITY

ROYAL LONDON

Queen Victoria's small diamond crown, made for the Queen in 1870 from the diamonds of a large necklace, is the tiniest of the crowns. It is 9.9cm in height and 9cm in diameter and became Victoria's trademark crown, appearing in countless portraits on top of her signature widow's cap. As a petite monarch, Victoria felt the Imperial Crown (above) to be a little cumbersome in which to conduct her royal duties. This miniature version was the solution. So attached was Her Majesty to this tiara-like crown that it was placed on her coffin at Osborne House.

The oldest and smallest pieces of the coronation regalia are the ampulla and spoon. Dating from the 12th Century, the ampulla and spoon are used to anoint a new monarch during the consecration stage of the coronation (see Chapter 7). The gold ampulla is a container for holy oil. Fashioned in the shape of an eagle, it has two holes in its beak through which the oil is poured. The silver-gilt spoon is then used to anoint the monarch on the breast, the backs of the hands and the forehead.

The old dictum that one can never have too many crowns is very much at play here in the Tower. St Edward's Crown is only worn once in the lifetime of a monarch – at the initial crowning ritual of the coronation. Notoriously heavy, weighing in at a neck-jeopardising 5 pounds or 2kg and made of solid gold adorned with 444 semi-precious stones, it too dates from the restoration and was made in 1661, although it is thought that some of its components may have come from an earlier, medieval crown.

There are three swords of state that are carried throughout the coronation. They are: the Curtana or Sword of Mercy, the blade of which is blunt and is symbolic of mercy; and the Swords of Spiritual and Temporal Justice – both of which are believed to have survived the Civil War because the Cromwellians were able to turn them to their practical purpose.

The sceptre symbolises the sovereign's worldly power under the cross. It was partly remade in 1910 to incorporate the largest cut diamond in the world, the First Star of Africa. The diamond weighs 535 carats and is almost as big as an ostrich egg. It was cut from the famed Cullinan diamond, which was given to King Edward VII at the beginning of the 20th Century as a birthday present by the South African Transvaal government just after the Boer War as a goodwill gesture. It beats socks.

With the sceptre comes the orb, given to the monarch by the Archbishop of Canterbury during the coronation to symbolise Christian sovereignty over the earth. A hollow sphere of gold, it is set with a mere 600 precious stones and pearls.

The sovereign's ring – a very different affair from a sovereign ring, thanks for asking – is placed on the fourth finger of the monarch's right hand and symbolises the marriage of monarch and state. The one we see here dates from the reign of King William IV in 1831.

The most modern piece is, paradoxically, the piece most steeped in legend. The Queen Mother's crown was made in 1937 for Elizabeth Bowes-Lyon for her coronation as Queen Consort to King George VI. It is made from solid platinum and set with nearly 3,000 diamonds. One of the most famous diamonds in history sits at the top of the crown.

The Koh-i-Noor diamond – the name means 'mountain of light' – dates back to the 16th Century and the Indian subcontinent. Described by Babur, first Mughal ruler of India, as worth half of the daily expense of the whole world, it was passed down from ruler to ruler.

It was presented to Queen Victoria as Empress of India by 10-year-old Maharajah Duleep Singh in 1849 following the annexation of the Punjab.

Legend maintains that the diamond will bring bad luck to any man that wears it and so since it arrived in Britain it has only been worn by women –Victoria, Queen Alexandra in 1902, and the last to wear it was the Queen Mum.

So that's M for museum. O for observatory refers to the site of the Royal Observatory, which was moved from here to Greenwich in 1675 – legend has it because the river fowl were gumming up the lenses of John Flamsteed's telescopes with guano.

Z for zoo seems more unorthodox, although some of the Tower's richest tales date from its life as a home for exotic beasts…

TEN TOWER MENAGERIE TALES

- ◼ *The Tower as a 'zoo' dates from the reign of King John.*
- ◼ *For over 600 years exotic beasts given as gifts by foreign heads of state were kept at the Tower.*
- ◼ *In 1251 there is record of the cost of the upkeep of King Henry III's polar bear.*
- ◼ *Records also show the construction of an elephant house in 1254.*
- ◼ *The Holy Roman Emperor once made a gift of three leopards for the menagerie.*
- ◼ *By the 18th Century the zoo was open to the public. The cost of admission was three and a half pence or a cat/dog with which to feed the lions.*
- ◼ *King James I had a platform built from which he and his chums could watch the lions fight each other and other animals for entertainment.*
- ◼ *1816 sees the arrival of the first grizzly bear in England, a gift of the Hudson Bay Company to King George III.*
- ◼ *The Lion Tower is so-named because of the lions that were once kept there.*
- ◼ *The animals had left the Tower by 1835, when they moved to Regent's Park, the current location of London Zoo.*

That the Tower was utilised as a royal armoury – the 'A' – is entirely appropriate and practically self-explanatory, given that the original Tower was such a flexing of military might in itself. But it is as a royal residence – the 'R' – that the Tower we see today takes physical shape.

The Tower of London as a royal residence

The Tower of London was the principal royal residence from when Willie came a-conquering right up until Harry came a-chopping: from King William I in 1066 to King Henry VIII in 1547.

To become a royal resident of the Tower of London wasn't always necessarily a good thing. Especially if your stay was to be a short one. Just ask Anne Boleyn. Or King Edward V. But more of them and their like later.

Let's begin, for a change, with the happy, domestic, un-bloody* side of royal domesticity. The kings and queens whose stay was characterised by freedom to leave the palace whenever they liked and whose lease wasn't, er, cut short give us nothing less than a half-a-millennium-long dynastic domestic makeover show.

The Tower was built in the reign of King William I with all mod cons. And all mod cans, too. The height of 11th-century sophistication – garderobes – can be found dotted around the edges of the central Great Hall.

These take the form of little closets with a seat, and below the seat a hole in the outside wall.

Can you guess what it is yet?

In the absence of plumbing, the royal waste products would literally fall out of the holes, run down the outside wall and into a pit dug below. Revolutionary stuff in a period when royal courtiers would simply relieve themselves wherever and whenever nature called. From this basic convenience we get the word wardrobe. This comes from the practice of hanging clothes in the garderobes because the vapour of the urine stopped fleas and moths nesting and destroying the fabric.

The Tower retained more or less its original proportions for the best part of a century, until the 10-year reign of that gallivanting evangelist Richard I. Richard I spent something in the region of £7,000 on castle-building during his time as king, some £2,800 of that sum being spent on the Tower. Money well spent? Well, yes and no. It was wise to fortify the Tower in the face of attack from Richard's brother Prince John. But then, having spent all the money, William Longchamp, Richard's Lord Chancellor, surrendered to John when he finally did attack in 1191.

The reigns of King Henry III and King Edward I saw expansion to almost the scale that we see today. Henry (1216–1272) was known as the Builder King and Edward (1272–1307) as a great warrior. Henry instigated the inner wall that

(*Well, comparatively un-bloody.)

surrounds the original White Tower (the actual Tower of London). Edward, not content with one wall, ordered the second curtain wall in the late 13th Century. Oh, and a moat, too. This was a man plainly aware of the number of enemies he had garnered.

Two successive kings, builder and warrior, bring the perfect alignment of the planets to create the imposing edifice on the Thames.

Right. Now it's 'T' time. Torture. Trials. Treason.

SOME SHORT-STAY RESIDENTS OF THE TOWER OF LONDON (SOME SHORTER THAN OTHERS)

KING HENRY VI

In 1465 Henry VI was captured during the dynastic struggle for supremacy known now as the Wars of the Roses. Brought to London, he was publicly humiliated and forced to process through the streets of the city on a lame horse.

Subjected to the jeers and heckles of a sneering mob at Islington (changed days: he'd be pelted with ciabatta today), he remained silent until someone punched him in the face, upon which intrusion he exclaimed: 'You do foully to smite a king anointed.' That's telling him.

Incarcerated in the Wakefield Tower for six years in far from five-star conditions, he remained there until Warwick the Kingmaker (see Chapter 4) freed him in 1470 and took him for a re-crowning at Westminster. That same North London chapter has already related Warwick's grisly fate, and Henry ended up back along the District Line banged up again.

On 21 May 1471 King Henry died in the Tower, contemporary opinion suggesting that he died from a broken heart on hearing news that his son had been killed in the Battle of Tewkesbury. Others suggest foul play.

Others often suggest foul play at the Tower, as we shall see…

The anniversary of his death is commemorated every year in the Ceremony of the Lilies and Roses, when white lilies are laid by Eton College pupils and white roses are laid by King's College pupils (both educational establishments were originally founded by Henry) in the chapel within Wakefield Tower.

In 1911 Henry's bones were disinterred from his grave at Chertsey Abbey and the back of the skull was found to be badly damaged… dun-dun-da-a-a-a-a-a-a-a-a-a-ah.

KING EDWARD V

Climbing the wooden stairs to enter the White Tower, one sees the recess where the old staircase once stood… and where in 1674 the bones of two little boys were discovered. Their bones were taken and buried in Innocents' Corner in Westminster Abbey.

They are believed to be the remains of the 12-year-old boy King Edward V and his 10-year-old brother Richard, Duke of York. Popular belief says that they were murdered in the Tower on the say-so of the man who would be King Richard III. Their deaths/disappearances, their lack of a recorded funeral, Shakespeare's hatchet job on King Dick, all conspire to make one of the saddest, most enduring mysteries of the whole royal saga.

LADY JANE GREY

The Nine Days' Queen was nominated as successor to Edward VI by the latter in his will. As such, she took up residence in the Tower of London. So when the wind changed and Queen Mary was appointed monarch, LJG was well placed for incarceration.

A little backstory: although King Edward VI agreed to change the order of succession on his deathbed in favour of the Protestant Lady Jane Grey, it was not the accepted norm while the king still had living siblings. This, coupled with the fact that his half-sister Mary was by birth right the next lawful monarch and daughter of the nation's beloved and much wronged Queen Catherine of Aragon, meant there was a groundswell of support for her on Edward's death. Shocked by the announcement that Lady Jane was to ascend the throne, Mary's supporters rallied round and she was proclaimed queen in Norwich. A week later Mary arrived in London with 13,000 clamouring for her coronation.

Even Lady Jane Grey's father realised the game was up and recognised Mary as queen and agreed to his daughter becoming a prisoner rather than guest at the Tower in a shocking change of heart.

On 3 August 1553 Mary made a triumphant entry into the city. She was never to be so popular again.

Aged 16, Lady Jane Grey was beheaded for high treason here at the Tower, and granted the privilege of a private execution behind the walls. Mere commoners and baddies were given the chop in public at Tower Hill.

The hauntingly vivid painting 'The Execution of Lady Jane Grey' by Paul Delaroche can be seen in the National Gallery.

ANNE BOLEYN

Second wife of King Henry VIII and first to suffer the drastic fate with which that king is so eternally associated, she was beheaded at Tower Green on 19 May 1536 – after which Henry VIII never spent a night at the Tower again.

A thousand days had elapsed since Anne had spent the eve of her coronation at the Tower. Her last request was for a French swordsman to perform the bloody task – English axemen were notoriously inaccurate and often took more than one swing at it to get the job done.

Anne failed in her task of giving Henry a son, but was mother to Queen Elizabeth I.

KATHERINE HOWARD

The fifth wife of Henry VIII met the same fate as wife number two, on 13 February 1542. Henry's beautiful teenage bride, a former lady-in-waiting, continued to write *billets-doux* to her lover Thomas Culpeper. Perhaps smarting from the old chestnut of there being no fool like an old fool (Henry was in his fifties), the ultimate sanction was wrought upon the unfaithful queen.

ROBERT DEVEREUX, EARL OF ESSEX

Last execution on the Green – as a war hero, a riot was feared if he were to be beheaded publicly. A former favourite of Queen Elizabeth I, he fell foul of her wrath when he led a plot to overthrow her.

The deed was done at 7am on 25 February 1601. Ever the showman, Bob was dressed to be killed, resplendent in black velvet and satin with a gold and red waistcoat. He confessed his sins to be 'more numerous than the hairs on his [soon-to-be-independent] head' and assumed the position, asking the axeman how best he should lay his head on the block. Not that this last question seemed to matter to the axeman, who took three swings to complete the task. His little black velvet number was ruined.

Devereux's was the last beheading on the Green. The last beheading at Tower Hill was of a fellow called Simon Fraser, the 11th Lord Lovat, executed in 1747 for his part in aiding the cause of the man he believed to be King Charles III… (Bonnie Prince Charlie).

ROYAL GUN SALUTES

To this day, royal gun salutes are fired at the Tower by the Honourable Royal Artillery.

- ■ *Four 25-pound guns are used.*
- ■ *The number of rounds fired depends on the occasion.*
- ■ *62-gun salutes are fired for royal occasions, the birthdays of the monarch/ consort and on the anniversary of the monarch's accession to the throne – this*

> is composed of 21 rounds for a royal salute, with 20 rounds because the Tower is a palace and another 21 to mark the City of London's unique status.
> ■ 41-gun salutes are fired for the State Opening of Parliament or on an official state visit.

The City of London

The City, the Square Mile, the financial capital of the UK, the oldest part of town. If relations with the monarchy are complex over in Westminster, they are positively labyrinthine out here.

Maybe it's got something to do with the fact that a queen once burned the whole place down.

Some 60 years after Christ, Boudicca,* Queen of the Iceni tribe who occupied what is more or less modern-day Norfolk, led a revolt against the occupying Romans and razed London to the ground. Her statue, a 19th-century affair no doubt attempting to hook Queen Victoria to the chariot of the powerful 1st-century warrior queen, can be found rampaging off her plinth, horses flying in battle-fuelled rage, at the northern end of Westminster Bridge. Some sources have it that Boudicca means 'victorious' and is therefore the close approximation of the modern name Victoria.

We must first separate the City of London from the city of London – note the lowercase 'c' in the latter. Rather like the Hungarian cities of Buda and Pest combining to make Budapest, London can also be divided into two cities. But where Buda and Pest are split by an east–west waterway, the conurbation that is now Greater London grew up and out of and around the old City. Thus the City of London forms the jam in the centre of the great big jammy dodger biscuit that is the urban sprawl we know today.

But where another famous queen – the White Queen in *Through the Looking-Glass* – offered Alice 'jam every other day', there's jam every day in the City of London, and plenty of it. The City of London is the richest square mile on God's green earth.

This 'independent city state' has sought no conflict with kings over borders and territorial power over the centuries. Instead, it has conquered the world through the tendrils of finance and business.

(*In recent decades the spelling and pronunciation of Boudicca have undergone something of a makeover. Formerly taught as Boadicea, the current spelling and pronunciation are believed to be the more accurate.)

In 1215 King John (he of Magna Carta and lesser Shakespeare History Play) granted the City a charter to elect its own lord mayor and corporation. The City of London Corporation is the name of the local authority that allows the Lord Mayor, the Court of Alderman and the Court of Common Council to run the City of London on its behalf.

Since 1215, they have very much been a closed shop to the monarch. Royalty, although duly acknowledged, has needed to show respect for this powerful centre of commerce. Perhaps Napoleon had a point when described us not as a nation of monarchs and subjects but as a nation of shopkeepers.

St Paul's Cathedral (2)

St Paul's Churchyard, EC4M 8AD. Tube: St Paul's

We enjoy referring to the City as the Old City – implying that Westminster, at a mere 1,000 years old, is actually just the baby part of town.

But one look around, one glance at the City, throws up an immediate anomaly: the Old City has all of our most modern buildings and looks utterly contemporary if not downright futuristic in places.

The exception is, of course, St Paul's Cathedral.

Wren's masterpiece still dominates the look of the City – if not the skyline – from afar.

Christopher Wren's famous dome, built in the aftermath of the Great Fire of London (there's no Royal London story connected to the central event of 1666: the royal court fled London, as it did one year earlier during the plague), still provides an architectural thrill. Three hundred and sixty-five feet tall to the cross atop the dome (second largest in Europe after St Peter's in Rome), this cathedral, actually the fourth to stand with the name St Paul's on this site, was opened by Queen Anne in the year 1710.

Queen Anne's statue stands outside the western porch of the cathedral – the 'front' of the building in the popular imagination – facing, as does the building, in a westerly direction. The statue is a 19th-century copy of the original statue by Francis Bird, erected in 1712. Its positioning seems both appropriate and innocuous today. But when it was first erected, it was the subject of much satire.

Back then, St Paul's faced west and was surrounded by a number of gin shops. Given the Queen's fondness for a libation or two (or three) and that her nickname was already Brandy Nan, those with an irreverent turn of mind found plenty to comment on, giving rise to the 18th-century rhyme:

Brandy Nan, Brandy Nan, you'll be left in the lurch
Your face to the gin shops, your back to the church

It has been observed that the proportions of the statue do something of a service to Queen Anne and something of a disservice to the truthfulness of the depiction. (As we have seen, art and artists have long been kind to our dear royals.) A woman of – how to put this delicately? – King Henry VIII-like proportions, much of her calorific intake being ingested in the aforementioned liquid form. By the end of her reign, it is said that she had gained such heft that the proportions of her coffin were more cuboid than rectangular.

As we have seen elsewhere in this book, Westminster Abbey is the royal church – but royalty has used St Paul's on a number of occasions for thanksgiving services, commemorations… and one rather memorable royal wedding.

In 1872 a thanksgiving ceremony was held here for Victoria for the recovery of her son Edward from typhoid – the illness that had taken her darling Prince Albert from her 11 years earlier. In 1897 another thanksgiving service was held at St Paul's to celebrate Victoria's 60th year as monarch, her Diamond Jubilee.

Famously, when Victoria's coach arrived at the bottom of the steps of the cathedral, Her Majesty was feeling a bit too old and stiff to climb them – it comes to us all. 'Old age,' as my dear, octogenarian Uncle Stu used to say, 'is not for wimps.'

To save Her Majesty the trouble, and perhaps the indignity, of surmounting the steps, the entire congregation and clergy flooded out and the service took place in the open air. An inscription carved into the paving remembers this event.

(A similar episode caught my eye during the coverage of the wedding of the Duke and Duchess of Cambridge on 29 April 2011. After the ceremony, the wedding guests left the Abbey. As the billions watched on, Prince Philip tried to gain access to the royal coach – quite a leap for a man of his senior years. HRH took one swing at it… and then another… and then… the TV director cut away to a shot of something else. Which was entirely the correct course of action. It is an undignified spectacle watching any nonagenarian trying to clamber into what is in effect a horse and cart. I think the director in question should be up for a badge – at least an MBE IMHO – soon.)

That Queen Victoria was unable to enter the cathedral seems a shame, given that she would not have been able to admire the newly installed colourful mosaics added to the ceiling roundels at the eastern end. This addition had been instigated after Her Maj had criticised St Paul's for being 'dreary, dingy and undevotional'. God moves in mysterious ways.

In the 20th Century, exactly 100 years on from the Great Exhibition (at which Prince Albert had been such a mover and shaker), King George VI opened the Festival of Britain from the steps of the cathedral. The King was in poor health, and it was one of his last public engagements.

Thirty years later, his grandson Prince Charles took a supporting role in the wedding of Lady Diana Spencer – at least that is how it is remembered by many.

THE WEDDING OF CHARLES AND DIANA

The royal wedding of 1981 was the biggest royal occasion for a generation. With the greatest respect to the investiture of the Prince of Wales in 1969 and the wedding of Princess Anne in 1973, it was the most important and the grandest royal occasion since the coronation of Queen Elizabeth II in 1953.

It took place on 29 July 1981.

The royal wedding credited by many as the catalyst for a degree of modernisation in the Royal Family has its roots in long-established tradition. Lady Diana Spencer was from just the right sort of family – an aristocrat, not a commoner like our Kate Middleton.

In terms of background, and the fact that the Prince had known Diana all her life, the union of Charles and Diana takes on aspects of an arranged marriage – although at the time such talk was banished in a hail of flash-bulbs and media coverage hailing the love story of the century. In terms of the vast timescale of our story, we must here remember that the previous love story of the century was still a recent and wounding event – King Edward VIII and Wallis Simpson.

The importance of the event in terms of it being a state occasion cried out for a larger venue than even the Abbey could provide – and Margaret Thatcher's government of the day elected for the greater capacity of St Paul's to accommodate the heads of state of the world in one of the biggest diplomatic headaches of recent decades.

The relationship of Charles and Diana has attracted an inordinate number of soothsayers down through the decades – a vast number of whom seem to have emerged since 1997 with the 20/20 vision that comes as standard with hindsight. 'Bad luck shall smite this union, it is surely a bad omen to break with the tradition of the Abbey.'

Applying hindsight from a sociological angle, the sheer scale of the day seems entirely in keeping with the excessive 1980s – 3,500 guests, the showy church… and the sheer acreage of Diana's dress.

THE TOWER OF LONDON AND THE CITY

ROYAL LONDON

DIANA SPENCER'S WEDDING DRESS

- Designed by David and Elizabeth Emanuel.
- Made of woven silk taffeta made by Stephen Walters of Suffolk.
- The train was 25 feet (7.62m) long – the length of nearly five King Charles Is (before beheading).
- Decorated with 10,000 pearls.
- The dress was valued at £9,000.

A royal wedding, when it is a state occasion, serves as a reminder that the UK is not the only country of the world that retains a fascination with monarchy. A glance at the 3,500 people on the guest list back in 1981 yields up the following ten royal invitees from elsewhere in the world. And this is just the tip of the iceberg…

- Her Serene Highness Princess Grace of Monaco (Grace Kelly)
- Their Majesties The King and Queen of the Belgians – King Baudouin and Queen Fabiola
- Their Majesties The King and Queen of the Bulgarians in exile – Simeon Saxe-Coburg and Gotha and Margarita Gómez-Acebo y Cejuela
- The Aga Khan IV
- Their Majesties The King and Queen of Tonga
- Their Majesties The King and Queen of Romania in exile – King Michael and Queen Anne
- Their Royal Highnesses the Crown Prince and Crown Princess of Jordan – Prince Hassan of Jordan and Princess Sarvath El Hassan
- His Royal Highness Prince Georg of Hanover
- His Majesty King Olaf V of Norway
- Her Royal Highness Princess Maha Chakri Sirindhorn of Thailand

Notable absentees on the above list are King Juan Carlos of Spain and Queen Sofia – who stayed away on the advice of the Spanish government. The British royal couple were due to depart on their honeymoon from Gibraltar – a territory the subject of dispute between Spain and the UK.

Temple Bar (3)

Paternoster Square, EC4M 7DX. Tube: St Paul's

Located just to the left of the western porch of St Paul's and acting as a graceful entrance to the renovated Paternoster Square stands Temple Bar. There is a pleasing continuity here – it is also the work of Wren.

But this is a very new home for Temple Bar. As its name suggests, it originally stood in the area known as Temple, home to the medieval warrior monks the Knights Templar until the early 14th Century. It was the original marker of the boundary between the City and Westminster. It stood at the western end of Fleet Street but was finally moved in 1878 because it was causing traffic congestion as horses and carriages tried to squeeze through the central arch.

It is first recorded as existing in 1293 and was rudimentary in the extreme, being merely a chain between two wooden posts. Since the days of Queen Elizabeth I, a short ceremony is always carried out at Temple Bar on state occasions when the monarch wishes to process through the City.

The lord mayor is summoned and the monarch then has to ask permission (the cheek!) to be admitted to the City, which is under the lord mayor's jurisdiction. The lord mayor symbolically offers the sword of state to show his loyalty and allegiance to the crown. The sword is then carried at the front of the royal procession to show that the sovereign is in the City under the lord mayor's protection.

This gate amazingly survived the Great Fire of 1666 but was replaced by Wren's design in the early 1670s.

The triple archway of white Portland stone features four royal statues. It is a celebration of the continuity of monarchy – conveniently ignoring that troublesome blip of the 11-year Commonwealth as there is no place for Cromwell. Wren has deliberately papered over the cracks of the Civil War with all the assurance that the restoration was permanent.

TEN STATUES AND CARVINGS OF MONARCHS AND CONSORTS IN THE CITY OF LONDON – ALL WITHIN A 10-MINUTE WALK OF ST PAUL'S

◼ *The statue of* **Queen Anne** *outside St Paul's (see above).*

◼ *The Temple Bar features four niches in which we remember:*

  ◼ **King James I**

  ◼ **Queen Anne of Denmark** *(James's wife)*

- King Charles I
- King Charles II

■ When the Temple Bar was relocated in the 1870s, it was replaced by a marker surmounted by a dragon – the fabled protector of the old City – designed by Horace Jones in 1880. Underneath the dragon – a further symbolic reminder? – we find statues of:

- Queen Victoria
- Edward IV

In addition, there is a carving of the then Prince of Wales – he faces east, looking ahead to the City and to his reign as **Prince Albert**.

■ **Queen Elizabeth I:** *the only central London statue of Queen Elizabeth I can currently be found on the church of St Dunstan-in-the-West – although she has been something of a gadabout down through the years. Dating from 1586, it ended up here following the demolition of Ludgate, its original location.*

■ **Mary, Queen of Scots:** *as in Westminster Abbey, it seems that Good Queen Bess can't turn a hair without Mary, Queen of Scots appearing by her side. Poetic justice? At 143–144 Fleet Street, a statue of the beheaded Scots monarch can be found, erected by 'an admirer' (Sir John Tollemache) around 1880.*

A NICE SIT DOWN AND A CUP OF TEA

On the main drag

New Armouries Café

Tower Green, Tower of London, EC3N 4AB. Tube: Tower Hill

Not a place one can swing by, given that it is actually within the confines of the Tower itself. But if you have already swung by the Tower, and if having a cup of tea where the axes swung by on the way to their appointments with royal necks is your cup of tea, then there's nowhere better.

The Tower also provides ample opportunity to take food away and find a corner in which to rest/perch and enjoy both the grub and the atmosphere. Perfect on a sunny day.

Something a little stronger, perhaps?

Skylounge Tower of London
DoubleTree by Hilton Hotel, 7 Pepys Street, EC3N 4AF. Tube: Tower Hill

Pricey? Oh yes. Bottled beers start at around £6. But the astonishing view of the Tower from the 12th-floor terrace is unforgettable.

Sssshhh. It's a secret

The Wine Library
43 Trinity Square, EC3N 4DJ. Tube: Tower Hill

The sign outside really does make it look more like a library than a place to imbibe, but this is a wine merchant with a difference. With a range of over 400 wines to choose from and a cellar restaurant in which to enjoy them, this independently owned business is less than five minutes from the Tower.

10 THE ROYAL WEST END

The West End of London is the capital's entertainment district. And while it could be suggested that entertainment aplenty can be had from royal-watching, what we mean is that this is the part of town where we come to enjoy ourselves. And as we have seen, some royals can enjoy themselves more than others.

Which brings us quite naturally to King Charles II. King Charles II loved the theatre... by which we mean he loved actresses.

Elsewhere in this book we have discussed royal pub names and (ahem) royal favourites. Here in the West End we can bring those two factors together – twice – in the shape of Nell Gwynne.

Nell Gwynne Tavern

1–2 Bull Inn Court, Strand, WC2R 0NP. Tube: Charing Cross/Embankment/ Covent Garden

The pub sign on this hidden hostelry, tucked no more than a dozen paces off the beaten track but still with a delicious, clandestine feel, features Nell in all her, er, glory. The sign is based on a work by Dutch Golden Age painter Simon Pietersz Verelst (he also painted Prince Rupert of the Rhine, see Chapter 8) – although in the pub sign version we seem to be treated to considerably less of La Gwynne's left nipple than in the original.

Nell of Old Drury

29 Catherine Street, WC2B 5JS. Tube: Covent Garden

Doesn't welcome walking tours even when quiet, but worth a quick look none-theless. The pub can be glimpsed in Hitchcock's *Frenzy* (1972) back when the district was in its fruit and veg market heyday.

It's probably too late now to reclaim top billing for the artistic gifts of Nell Gwynne over her sexual reputation, but I feel it's the decent thing to keep trying.

In the 'new' theatre, brought back to life after the restoration of the monarchy, women played female roles for the first time – young boys had played them hitherto. Gwynne's particular talent lay in playing the female half of the 'gay

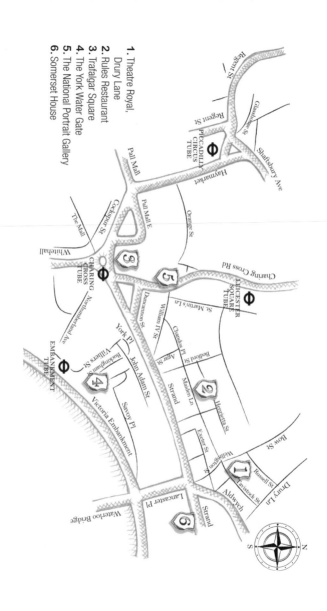

1. Theatre Royal, Drury Lane
2. Rules Restaurant
3. Trafalgar Square
4. The York Water Gate
5. The National Portrait Gallery
6. Somerset House

couple', the male of whom would display rakish tendencies, with the woman protesting her virtue too much. These bawdy, broad restoration comedies still bring the house down in the 21st Century, and Gwynne was described by writer Elizabeth Howe as 'the most famous Restoration actress of all time, possessed of an extraordinary comic talent' in her book *The First English Actresses*.

Gwynne's theatrical career began as an orange seller – the fruit with which she is so associated in the popular imagination. The orange sellers would, of course, sell oranges to the theatregoers but also relay messages backstage to the actresses who may have caught the eye of the gentlemen (I use the term advisedly) in the auditorium.

Gwynne gave birth to two sons, Charles (1670) and James (1671), fathered by King Charles II. James died aged ten. Charles became the first Duke of St Albans. It is said that this latter title was only coined to stop Nell referring to the child as 'the Little Bastard' in the presence of the King. 'I have nothing else to call him by!' she would protest. Rather than chanting 'sticks and stones' at his disgruntled mistress, the King created a dukedom.

Theatre Royal, Drury Lane (1)

Catherine Street, WC2B 5JF. Tube: Covent Garden

The Theatre Royal, Drury Lane (actually in Catherine Street) has occupied this spot since 1663 when King Charles II granted one Thomas Killigrew permission to stage 'legitimate drama'.

The current building is the fourth such theatre on the site and dates from 1812 (with the interior renovated in 1922 into the opulent auditorium we enjoy today). Previous Theatre Royals had burned down in 1672, been demolished in 1791, and burned down again in 1809.

'Legitimate drama' is seldom the order of the day at the Theatre Royal these days. Straight plays have taken something of a back seat to musicals here since the Second World War, from Rodgers and Hammerstein's *The King and I* to the musical of Mel Brooks's *The Producers*.

My Fair Lady, book by Alan Jay Lerner and music by Frederick Loewe, enjoyed its London premiere here in 1958, running for 2,281 performances. A musical version of Shaw's *Pygmalion*, it starred Rex Harrison as Professor Higgins.

Harrison is the subject of one of the more persistent theatrical myths, which relates that he is the illegitimate son of King Edward VII. The musical features a famous scene at Ascot racecourse which, in the film (also starring Harrison) is costumed by Cecil Beaton as 'Black Ascot' – the famous Derby race meeting held in the wake of the death of King Edward VII in 1910, in which racegoers dressed in the colours of mourning.

TEN WEST END THEATRES WITH ROYAL CONNECTIONS

Prince of Wales Theatre
Coventry Street, W1D 6AS. Tube: Piccadilly Circus
Built in 1884 (the version we see today dates from 1937) and named after the future King Edward VII. In 1963, The Beatles played the Royal Variety Performance here, in the presence of Queen Elizabeth, the Queen Mother. John Lennon's exhortation that those in 'the cheap seats, clap your hands; the rest of you can just rattle your jewellery' was received in the spirit of impish humour rather than sedition. Backstage, legend has it, in the royal line-up, the Queen Mother asked where the group were playing next. When informed that The Fabs' next gig was to be Slough, she is said to have replied, 'Oh, that's near us,' a reference to Windsor Castle's proximity.

The London Palladium
Argyle Street, W1F 7TF. Tube: Oxford Circus
Widely regarded to be the pinnacle of British show business, it was here on 3 November 1952 that Queen Elizabeth II attended her first Royal Variety Performance with the Duke of Edinburgh. The bill included Tony Hancock and Norman Wisdom. It was on the way to the Royal Variety Performance in late 2010 that demonstrators protesting against student fees assailed the Rolls-Royce Phantom VI carrying the Princes of Wales and the Duchess of Cornwall.

The Palace Theatre
Shaftesbury Avenue, W1D 8AY. Tube: Leicester Square
As its scale would suggest, this grand Victorian theatre was originally intended to be an opera house. The venue of the first Royal Variety Performance in 1912 in the presence of HRH King George V and Queen Mary. They were entertained by George Robey ('The Prime Minister of Mirth') and Harry Lauder.

Victoria Palace Theatre
Victoria Street, SW1E 5EA. Tube: Victoria
Designed by Frank Matcham, the Victoria Palace saw the original production of Me and My Girl open in 1937. When King George VI and Queen Elizabeth attended, it was noted that the royal couple joined in on the 'Oi!' responses during the show's

most famous number 'The Lambeth Walk', a tune described by the Nazis as 'Jewish mischief and animalistic hopping'.

The Empire
Leicester Square, WC2H 7NA. Tube: Leicester Square
Opened as a theatre in 1884, the Empire began showing films by the Lumière brothers in 1896. The first Royal Command Film Performance was shown here in 1946 (see Chapter 3).

The Prince Edward Theatre
Old Compton Street, W1D 4HS. Tube: Leicester Square/Tottenham Court Road
Built in 1930 and named after the then Prince Edward, Prince of Wales, who would become (albeit briefly and without coronation) King Edward VIII.

Duke of York's Theatre
St Martin's Lane, WC2N 4BG. Tube: Leicester Square
Opened as the Trafalgar Theatre, renamed in 1895 after the man who would become King George V.

Playhouse Theatre
Northumberland Avenue, WC2N 5DE. Tube: Charing Cross
Snoo Wilson's play HRH, directed by Simon Callow, opened here on 2 September 1997. Its theme was the Duke and Duchess of Windsor, the abdicated King Edward VIII and Wallis Simpson. In the immediate aftermath of the death of Diana, Princess of Wales it was harshly reviewed as anti-royal. The Playhouse was also home to The Goon Show, the BBC radio comedy so beloved of Prince Charles. Who else but Spike Milligan, the creative genius at the heart of the team, would be allowed to call the Prince of Wales a 'Little grovelling bastard' when HRH paid Spike a glowing tribute at an award ceremony?

The London Coliseum
St Martin's Lane, WC2N 4ES. Tube: Leicester Square/Charing Cross
Completed in 1902, the London Coliseum is still the West End's largest theatre with 2,359 seats. It had all sorts of advanced technical wizardry, including London's very first revolving stage to aid the speed at which acts could follow on from one another, and the unique 'King's Car' described in the programme thus...

> *'Immediately upon entering the theatre, the Royal Party will step into a richly furnished lounge which, at a signal, will move softly along a track formed in*

the floor, and into a large foyer which contains the entrance to the Royal Box. The King's Car remains at the entrance to the box and serves as an ante-room during the performance.'

It all sounds wonderfully sophisticated. However...
The King's Car was only used once, when King Edward VII was treated to its luxuries. All went well until the lever was pulled for the car to move and the fuse blew with a bang and the car refused to budge an inch. Edward emerged roaring with laughter and walked to his seat in the royal box.

The Vaudeville Theatre
Strand, WC2R 0NH. Tube: Charing Cross
The stage door – and royal entrance – is situated on Maiden Lane, on the estate of the Duke of Bedford, was once gated at one end with a statue of the Virgin Mary at the other. Queen Victoria found this most inconvenient for her driver when trying to turn her coach and requested of Bedford that the gate be removed.

Rules Restaurant (2)

35 Maiden Lane, Covent Garden WC2E 7LB. Tube: Charing Cross/Covent Garden

Maiden Lane is home to London's oldest restaurant, Rules, established in 1798 and a favoured haunt of naughty old King Ted no. 7 and his – here we go again – great favourites, a series of women referred to by his wife Queen Alexandra as 'the Horizontals'.

Rules specialises in traditional English fayre and in the 19th Century boasted the most exclusive 'table for two' in town. Behind the first-floor lattice window on the right of the main door was where the Prince of Wales, future King Edward VII, would secretly wine and dine his mistress the ravishing actress Lillie Langtry. There was even a secret side door created so that the couple could come and go undetected by other diners.

When Edward VII had her presented to the royal court and to his mother Queen Victoria, Langtry rather cheekily wore a headdress with three tall ostrich plumes, daringly mimicking the Prince of Wales's crest. During his time as PoW, it is said that Queen Victoria feared for the continuity of the monarchy, such was her heir's free-and-easy behaviour. Even at Edward's coronation, there were seats set aside for three of his mistresses in the balcony or clerestory of the Abbey. Some commented on this, calling the balcony Edward's Loose Box.

Trafalgar Square (3)

Tube: Charing Cross

The royal history of Trafalgar Square goes back to the reign of King Edward I when what is now the northern side of the square was used as a place to keep the royal hawks and horses – the royal mews.

And even in the 21st Century, Trafalgar Square is immediately readable as a clear statement of imperial intent. Lions and heroes and kings, oh my! (to borrow from *The Wizard of Oz*).

The bronze lions are the work of Sir Edwin Landseer, an artist beloved of Queen Victoria herself and from whom she often commissioned portraits of her family and pets. Above the lions, Nelson sits atop his famous column, one of very few contexts where a 'commoner' is elevated above the monarchy.

Some 176 feet below and behind the great naval hero, to his left shoulder we find an equestrian statue of King George IV. The great Francis Chantrey brings us the handsome figure of 'Prinny' on horseback. In life, such a horse would have required a robust constitution given that the king often had trouble passing a pie.

To the west of the king on horseback is the square's most famous, most talked-about, most controversial plinth – the fourth, or the 'empty' plinth. Originally, the plinth was reserved for an equestrian statue of King William IV, but funding for the project was found to be insufficient on the King's death.

Over the years a number of candidates have been proposed for the plinth. Diana, Princess of Wales was one such suggestion; Nelson Mandela another, given the proximity of South Africa house and the anti-apartheid demonstrations that took place in the square during the 1980s. But in 2008 it was reported that the plinth was reserved for another equestrian statue – the design is, after all, symmetrical, and a second equestrian statue would balance the square perfectly. The subject of the statue, the report said, was to be Queen Elizabeth II and work would commence upon her death. At the time, a GLA spokesperson told the *Daily Mail*: 'We will not enter into speculation about the long-term future of the fourth plinth, but the GLA is concerned with managing the successful rolling programme of contemporary art.'

Since 2008, the story of the Queen's statue has disappeared and the rolling programme of contemporary art has taken up residence on the fourth plinth. Sir Keith Park, the man charged with the air defence of London during the war, was commemorated here before being moved to a permanent berth outside the Athenaeum Club. And, in 2009, Anthony Gormley's *Fourth Plinth* project offered everyone the opportunity to be king for a day by allowing members of the public to 'book in' to a slot to act as a living statue.

A final kingly statue, however, can be found in Trafalgar Square. King James II in Roman garb can be found just outside the western end of the portico of the National Gallery. The last Catholic king of England, James II's belief in the Divine Right of Kings, the same business that got his old man Charles I into such hot water, saw him emerge as a threat to the established order. When his son-in-law William landed an invading army from the Netherlands, James fled into exile in France and William was crowned as the third king of that name, with his wife, James's daughter, as Queen Mary II. With the Jacobite forces defeated at the Battle of the Boyne in 1690, James lived out his days as a pretender to the throne in exile.

The current positioning of his statue (credited to Grinling Gibbons) is the fourth such berth it has occupied in London, having also stood in Whitehall and St James's Park. One can't help wondering that if the Queen Elizabeth equestrian statue business turns out to be true, then will it be appropriate to have King James II seemingly tiptoeing up behind the Defender of the Faith in Trafalgar Square?

At the southernmost side of the square, we find another equestrian statue, that of Jimmy II's dear old dad, King Charles I. At its, erm, hindquarters, a plaque set in the flagstones attests that this is the dead centre of London. This plaque was required when civil servants were given an extra living allowance to account for the additional expense of living in a six-mile radius of central London. With this plaque, there was no fiddling of the expenses.

The statue of King Charles is the oldest thing on display in the square, dating from 1633, and hidden at the end of the English Civil War. During the Second World War the statue was taken down and put in a safe place. Presumably the removal of the king's head with an axe in 1649 was ignominious enough, and letting his head get blown off all over again by the Luftwaffe would just have added insult to injury.

The statue, in turn, stands on the spot where the Eleanor Cross once stood – the replica monument, now called Charing Cross, stands just a few hundred yards to the east of the original site.

The Eleanor Crosses were erected on the say-so of King Edward I upon the death of his beloved Queen Eleanor, who died in Northamptonshire in 1290. Twelve crosses were erected to mark the route of the funeral procession to the Abbey. Three survive – one at Waltham Cross, another (the best preserved original) at Geddington, and one in Northampton. But the most famous is the 19th-century version at Charing Cross.

Charing was named after the ancient village that once stood at the bend in the River Thames ('charing' is old Saxon for bend or turn in the river). The cross that can be seen today stands before the Charing Cross Hotel, just to the east of Trafalgar Square at the start of the Strand. Resembling nothing less than the spire of some vast, underground cathedral, it dates from 1865 and was commissioned by the South Eastern Railway – the artist was Edward Middleton Barry – to act as the centerpiece of the forecourt at their grand new railway terminus.

The York Water Gate (4)

Victoria Embankment Gardens, WC2N 6NA. Tube: Embankment

The River Thames, as well as being a healthier and far less busy waterway today, is also a lot less wide, having been embanked in the 1860s (see Chapter 7). Its former width at Charing Cross can be gauged by the position of the York Water Gate, attributed to Inigo Jones, a Grade I listed structure, which was once the riverside entrance to the home of the Bishop of York (the site had been the property of the Bishops of Norwich until King Henry VIII's time).

In the 1620s it became the London home of George Villiers, the Duke of Buckingham – nearby Villiers and Buckingham Streets are named in his memory. Villiers was the great favourite of King James I (and VI). His portrait can be found back in Trafalgar Square at the National Portrait Gallery. The picture captures his favourite feature – his lovely, long legs – in all their glory.

The National Portrait Gallery (5)

St Martin's Place, WC2H 0HE. Open daily 10am–6pm, Thu/Fri till 9pm. Admission free. Tube: Charing Cross*

TEN KINGS AND QUEENS IN THE NATIONAL PORTRAIT GALLERY

If you're on a whistle-stop tour, these are the ones to see.

KING RICHARD III BY AN UNKNOWN ARTIST, LATE 16TH CENTURY

A portrait that proves the dictum: the victors write history. The crookback villain of Shakespeare's play is here captured looking a rather worried man. Milky, almost. That he plays with his gold ring is no doubt to signal to us, if we had forgotten, of his wealth and power. The effect, however, is more that of a man who can't remember if he's switched the gas off before leaving the house. An illuminating look behind the myth.

QUEEN MARY I BY MASTER JOHN, 1544

Master John seems to be aiming for demure… but the eyes have steel in them, and there's determination in those thin lips. Queen Mary's nickname to history? Bloody Mary.

QUEEN ELIZABETH I BY MARCUS GHEERAERTS THE YOUNGER, 1592

Serene, despite the elements gathering about her, clad in virginal white and standing square in the heart of her realm, this great hagiographic portrait of Good Queen Bess was commissioned from Gheeraerts by Sir Henry Lee of Ditchley. The Queen's great favourite Robert Devereux, Earl of Essex was also one of Gheeraerts' subjects.

*The collection at the NPG is rotated regularly and some works may not be on display when you visit. If this is the case, you can make use of the NPG's wonderful computerised archive, Portrait Explorer, on the ground-floor mezzanine (nice, comfy chairs, too!) and browse the portraits that the gallery lacks space to have on view.

KING JAMES I BY DANIEL MYTENS, 1621

King James cuts a melancholy monarch in this portrait, despite his finery, his regal red robes. Is it the strain of dealing with Parliament showing in his sad eyes? Or is it that they've positioned him for posterity in such a pose that he can't see the well-turned ankle of his great favourite the Duke of Buckingham (see below)?

KING CHARLES I BY DANIEL MYTENS, 1631

Ten years on from the portrait of his father, Mytens again brings out the melancholy in the royal gaze. But here, hindsight gives the look a tone of resignation rather than sadness. The trappings of monarchy are all around him – the crown to his right hand, opulent red drapes adorn his room. Do his blue clothes allude to the Virgin Mary and the Divine Right of Kings? Similarly, the glimpse of the blue sky in the background: his heaven-sent right to be absolute monarch?

KING CHARLES II BY THOMAS HAWKER, C1680

This king has a look of a man who labours under an almost pathological inability to deny himself even the smallest pleasure. And by 1680, when the King was 50 years of age, it was starting to show. And bear in mind that the artist may have been, er, overlooking certain signs of overindulgence. The double chin is creeping in – and if it's creeping in in an oil painting, what was it doing in life? If I were in an uncharitable mood I might even go so far as to say he looks seedy. A vivid study in overindulgence.

QUEEN ANNE BY MICHAEL DAHL, 1705

Art and artists have long been kind to our dear royals. And this is no more in evidence than in this portrait of Queen Anne. By all accounts a larger lady – buried, famously, in an almost cube-shaped coffin, as we have seen – Dahl's portrait captures her as such. But, as with King Charles above, if Dahl is aiming for somewhere between big-boned and Rubenesque, what would a camera have caught had such a thing been around?

KING GEORGE IV BY AN UNKNOWN ARTIST AFTER SIR THOMAS LAWRENCE, 1815

The storm clouds of war gather all around, but all they can do is tousle the King's hair into a coiffure that would be the envy of any boyband. Again, this heroic figure of a fellow may not necessarily be 100% accurate, particularly in terms of girth. (We are reminded of Beau Brummell's archly cutting remark, 'Who's your fat friend?' aimed at George when he was Prince of Wales.) It has been suggested that Prinny was feeling a little left out of the military shenanigans in the continental Europe of the day, and wanted to play at soldiers with the best of 'em – hence the costume and setting of this portrait.

KING WILLIAM IV BY SIR MARTIN ARCHER SHEE, C1800

An actual sailor this time – Sailor Bill was one of his nicknames – King William IV looks perfectly at home among the swirl of smoke and the ensign of the navy, his cheeks reddened not from overindulgence (see Charles, above) but from the exertions of war.

QUEEN VICTORIA BY SIR GEORGE HAYTER, 1863

Sir George Hayter catches both a young queen and the 21st-century gallery-goer off guard. Where we often expect the older version of the popular imagination, here we have the young queen who took the throne at the age of just 18. Like the portrait of King Richard III (above) it challenges the popular perception of the monarch and encourages the modern onlooker to consider the Queen from a different angle.

TEN ROYAL CAMEO ROLES, BADDIES, SUPPORTERS AND LOVERS IN THE NATIONAL PORTRAIT GALLERY

If you've abandoned your whistle-stop tour because you've fallen in love with the National Portrait Gallery and are going to throw away your tickets to We Will Rock You *and stay and enjoy the paintings instead, then these are the next ten to see… **

Thomas Cranmer by Gerlach Flicke, 1545

Instrumental in Henry VIII's divorce from Catherine of Aragon, Cranmer's dark, wide eyes stare into the middle distance as if in contemplation of the scriptures – a bible is open in his hands and important-looking documents lie nearby.

Flora Macdonald by Richard Wilson, 1747

Again an illuminating reminder that there are two sides to every story. Those who are over-fond of tales of Scottish heroism being peopled by small Australian actors with blue faces need only look at this portrait: calm, even serene, this is a woman whose self-possession and sense of duty needs no Hollywood makeover

Bonnie Prince Charlie by Louis Gabriel Blanchet, 1738

Roguishly referred to by one of my Scots London Walks colleagues as King Charles III, he is captured here in another portrait that may cause great surprise to those of you who have seen Braveheart too often. Bewigged, rouged of cheek, striking a pose that suggests nothing less than a man who is just about to bust a few moves on Strictly Come Dancing… And small, too. Perhaps even smaller than diminutive Australian actor Mel Gibson, who donned the blue face paint to play William Wallace, his spiritual antecedent, in the aforementioned Braveheart.

Prince Rupert, attributed to Gerrit van Honthorst, c1641
He still looks like an early 1970s rock musician. Very soulful eyes.

George Villiers, 1st Duke of Buckingham, attributed to William Larkin, c1616
It's all in the legs. Villiers believed himself to be in possession of the finest and most attractive pins in the kingdom.

Wallis Simpson, Duchess of Windsor by Gerald Leslie Brockhurst, 1939
A love story to beat all others? A priggish fop with a bullyish penchant for the wives of other men? The story of Edward and Mrs Simpson still has the power to enthral. And here at the National Portrait Gallery there are a number of photographic studies of the wicked woman in question which will also do just that. Not a conventional beauty, but certainly strikingly handsome. We've been combing through her photographs now for generations, looking for clues as to why the King would give it all up. Richard Avedon's photograph of the Duchess with her beloved Edward from 1957 has the melancholy air of an old-time vaudeville act only half remembered by their once-adoring public. Cecil Beaton, 20 years earlier, captures more of a star-crossed lovers element to the couple. Away from her famous husband, in Gerald Brockhurst's oil on canvas from 1939, she seems angular, feline and beguiling indeed. Which is the real Duchess? I suspect that all of them are, in their own way.

Oliver Cromwell by Robert Walker, c1649
Cor, 'e's like the spectre at the feast, ain't 'e just? History, again, is painted by the victors, as this perfectly reasonable figure of middle England looks us clear in the eye with all the assurance of one with God on his side. Not smiling, suffice to say.

Barbara Palmer (née Villiers), Duchess of Cleveland with her son, Charles Fitzroy (as Madonna and Child) by Sir Peter Lely, 1664
'Mistress of King Charles II' is hardly an elite club – but this portrait perhaps tells the tale of the woman whose title of 'Mistress of KCII' is often prefixed with 'the Most Important', 'the Most Beautiful' or 'the Most Influential'. The look in her eye, as she brandishes the king's illegitimate son like a trophy, is certainly one of the cat who has

got the cream. Gave the King five illegitimate children and picked up the nickname 'the Uncrowned Queen' along the way. On the wedding day of Charles and Catherine of Braganza, she hung her undergarments in the palace grounds for all to see. Samuel Pepys, never far from getting overheated on such matters, gives us this account:

'In the Privy Gardens saw the linen petticoats of my Lady Castlemayne laced with the richest lace at the bottom, that I ever saw, and it did me good to look upon them.'

Maria Fitzherbert by Sir Joshua Reynolds, 1786–1788

'Morganatic' is one of those words that royal experts tend to brandish like peacock feathers to signify that they are not merely watching a good old soap opera along with the rest of us. Defined as 'of or denoting a marriage in which neither the spouse of lower rank nor any children have any claim to the possessions or title of the spouse of higher rank' it is a term that always crops up in conjunction with Maria Fitzherbert. One of the great beauties of the age, her morganatic marriage to King George IV went unrecognised as she was Catholic, and she occupied the status of mistress in the eyes of the law when the King married Caroline of Brunswick.

Louise de Kéroualle, Duchess of Portsmouth by Pierre Mignard, 1682

Mistress of… guess who? Her position as mistress was encouraged by the French government as a, 'ow you say, tool of diplomacy. She is pictured with a black slave girl whose presence serves to remind us of the Duchess's status.

Somerset House (6)

Strand, WC2R 1LA. Tube: Temple/Charing Cross/Embankment

The Somerset House we know and love today – Sir William Chambers' masterpiece from the late 18th Century with Victorian additions – has both hidden and housed episodes of great rebellion in our royal story.

The current structure, begun in 1776, occupies a site upon which a royal residence had stood for more than two centuries prior to this. The Duke of Somerset, Edward VI's Lord Protector, built an imposing palace here; before becoming Queen Elizabeth I, plain old Princess Elizabeth used the palace.

In the 17th Century the palace was used by the queens of King James I (indeed, his bride, Anne of Denmark, gave rise to the palace being renamed Denmark House) and Charles I and II. It was the religious practices of Catherine of Braganza, wife of King Charles II, that saw the place gain a reputation as a hotbed of Catholic conspiracy. This conspiracy was central to Titus Oates's fabricated Popish Plot of 1678.

NINE ROYAL FINGERPRINTS ON THE MODERN-DAY STREETS OF THE WEST END

Orange Street, WC2
A slightly more oblique royal reference than the one most apparent – William of Orange. The orange in question here is the principal colour of the coat of arms of the Duke of Monmouth, eldest illegitimate son of King Charles II. This southern extremity of his land – his palace helped form what is now Soho Square – was where he kept his stables.

Villiers Street
Named after George Villiers, Duke of Buckingham.

Charles II Street
Completed in 1689 on land developed by the Earl of St Albans, Henry Jermyn (the founding father of modern St James's). It was known as plain old Charles Street until as recently as 1939.

Kingsway
Named after King Edward VII, this long, wide street, in tandem with Aldwych, cleared away many a music hall, drinking den and house of ill repute from the London map in the early 20th Century. Given the nature of the goings-on here in former days, some have commented on the ironic nature of naming the new road after our good-time king.

Regent Street
One of the most famous shopping streets in all of London bends its elegant progress from Piccadilly to All Souls Church. It is still associated with the great John Nash, although the only building of his that survives is the aforementioned church. Every building is preserved as a listed building of one grade or another and the street is named after the Prince Regent, later King George IV.

Essex Street, WC2
Marks the location of a riverside mansion, a favourite of Queen Elizabeth I.

Burleigh Street, WC2
The location of another of Elizabeth I's favourite mansions.

William IV Street, WC2
A street the colour of public school refectory custard built in the reign of the king after which it is named. Once home to the Charing Cross Hospital, the Metropolitan Police now occupy the building.

Hanover Square, W1
Named after the Royal House of Hanover 1714–1901; first monarch King George I, last monarch Queen Victoria.

Savoy Place
The Savoy Hotel – the first hotel to be lit throughout by electricity – could count King Edward VII among its guests. Its name goes a long way further back, however, than the foundation of the hotel in 1889. The Savoy Palace that stood here until 1381 – when it was destroyed in the Peasants' Revolt (see Chapter 6) – was considered to be the grandest of all medieval residences. In the 14th Century it was the property of John of Gaunt, uncle of Richard II.

A NICE SIT DOWN AND A CUP OF TEA

Finding somewhere to sit down and have a cup of something in the West End is every bit as simple as digging up traces of the monarchy in North London was tough (see Chapter 4)

Of our three categories, well, it's safe to say that they are all pretty much on the main drag - it's just that some of them are more prominent than others.

On the main drag

The Sherlock Holmes Pub

10-11 Northumberland Avenue, WC2N 5DB. Tube: Embankment

This pub is one of the most touristy in town and is always very busy. But then show me a pub that's quiet every night in central London and I'll show you a pub that will soon be turned into a Starbucks. Busy pubs are busy for a reason and this one has the wonderfully eccentric Sherlock Holmes exhibit upstairs, as well as fine fish and chips and sundry other English fare in the restaurant.

As you leave the restaurant, go straight out of the door at the bottom of the stairs. Look up, above the anonymous five exit doors immediately before you, and you'll see some eastern-flavoured tilework. This is the former entrance of the Northumberland Avenue Turkish bath - where Holmes and Watson discreetly discuss the details of their Illustrious Client (mentioned earlier in Chapter 8). In the upstairs restaurant itself you can find the aforementioned Sherlock Holmes exhibit - a 'lifesize model' of the great detective's study. Look closely and you will see the initials VR shot into the wall with bullets. Holmes, great establishment man that he is, has paid tribute to the monarch while indulging in a spot of shooting practice.

Great detective, loyal monarchist, lousy next-door neighbour.

Something a little stronger, perhaps?

Gordon's Wine Bar

47 Villiers Street, WC2N 6NE. Tube: Embankment

Gordon's Wine Bar is a London legend. This cellar bar, with its faux-dingy décor and false cobwebs, was once described as resembling the venue at which Miss Havisham held her hen night. The walls are adorned with old newspaper cuttings and front pages, many of them featuring big royal events. Founded in 1890, it is the oldest wine bar in London.

Sssshhh. It's a secret

The Café in the Crypt

St Martin-in-the-Fields, Trafalgar Square, WC2N 4JJ. Tube: Charing Cross/Leicester Square

Okay, it's hardly a secret: the Café in the Crypt is a beloved rest-and-be-thankful of countless Londoners. But it is a hidden gem in the respect that it is the café beneath a wondrous classical church by James Gibbs. A great, affordable menu, wonderful nooks and corners in which to sit down and have a read, masses of London Walks leaflets to grab on the way in/out. And you're in and around the spot where King Edward I kept his stables (see page 165).

THE KINGS AND QUEENS OF ENGLAND

A quick who's who

William I: 1066–1087

Duke of Normandy, William the Bastard, victor at the Battle of Hastings 1066 and all that. Steely, focused, a man with a mission – our Conqueror King.

William II: 1087–1100

Nicknamed Rufus – the Redhead – and best remembered for his unexpected death. He was shot by an arrow while out hunting in the New Forest.

Henry I: 1100–1135

Henry the Just, Henry the Fair, he had meticulous administrative skills – he firmed up the Norman dynasty and put in place in the modern legal system.

Stephen: 1135–1154

Friendly but ineffectual, Stephen was thwarted by Henry's daughter, Matilda, who wanted to be queen. Stephen eventually agreed that her son should succeed him and then obediently died.

Henry II: 1154–1189

Hot-tempered, impetuous, the first of the Plantagenet kings, Henry is blamed for the gruesome death of Thomas Becket, much-loved Archbishop of Canterbury.

Richard I: 1189–1199

The Lionheart, the Crusading King, outstanding warrior. Richard was in fact an absent monarch, only spending six months of his 10-year reign in England.

John: 1199–1216

Bad King John, villain of the Robin Hood story, thoroughly nasty piece of work by all accounts. His high-handed behaviour with aristocracy led to them compiling the Magna Carta, which he was forced to agree to in 1215.

Henry III: 1216–1272

The Builder King, much enamoured with all things French. He had Westminster Abbey rebuilt to reflect his taste.

Edward I: 1272–1307

Longshanks, the Hammer of the Scots, Father of the English Legal System. A warlord extraordinaire, unflinchingly cruel. His final wish was to be buried in a simple wooden tomb, so that if the Scots should rise up then his bones were easily obtainable to be carried in front of the English army to suppress them once again.

Edward II: 1307–1327

As is so often the case, the uninterested son runs the family business into the ground. The antithesis of his Dad, Edward with his butterfly mind let his heart rule his head and his obsession with favourite Piers Gaveston dominate his legacy.

Edward III: 1327–1377

Charming and handsome, it was Edward who promoted the prototype English gentleman through chivalry and good manners and being polite to the ladies.

Richard II: 1377–1399

Vain, arrogant and lavishly well dressed, Dick 2 is credited with popularising the handkerchief but his petulant pride led to his deposition during the Wars of the Roses.

Henry IV: 1399–1413

Ruthless and tenacious, Henry spent his energies trying to hold onto the crown during the turbulent battles of the Wars of the Roses. His enemies were chopped up and their bodies brought to London so that limbs and heads could be displayed on skewers on London Bridge.

Henry V: 1413–1422

The Hero King – winner of Agincourt. Henry had a natural flair for kingship but died prematurely, not heroically in battle but of dysentery.

Henry VI: 1422–1461

Henry the Holy, Henry the Humble – a man too good to be king. He was dethroned and imprisoned twice and died in the Tower... some say through treachery.

Edward IV: 1461–1483
Gallant, graceful and gifted, at six feet tall he was every inch the fairytale king who would be able to end the Wars of the Roses. But he was betrayed by his friend the Earl of Warwick and then his own brother, the Duke of Clarence. Edward could be tough – he had his brother drowned in a barrel of Malmsey wine, reputedly his favourite tipple.

Edward V: 1483
Tragic, 12-year-old boy king who was allegedly murdered in the Tower alongside his brother.

Richard III: 1483–1485
Maligned as the crookback baddie by Shakespeare, said to have ordered the murder of the two Princes in the Tower in order to take the crown himself. Last of the York kings.

Henry VII: 1485–1509
Cunning, crafty and ferociously ambitious, the son of a minor Welsh nobleman, Henry scaled the dizzy heights of the monarchy. The last king to win the crown by force, he was also a talented housekeeper and kept a tight hold on the privy purse and created royal stability for the first time in a hundred years.

Henry VIII: 1509–1547
Transformed the course of British history by divorcing his first wife. Possibly the most infamous king of all time.

Edward VI: 1547–1553
Serious and rather sickly, Edward became king at just nine years old. A puppet king dominated by his fiercely ambitious Protestant Lord Protector, Somerset, he never ruled independent of his elders, dying at just 16 of consumption. His reign would have been a big disappointment to his father after he had gone to such extremes to sire him.

Mary I: 1553–1558
Bloody Mary reigned for just five years during which time she had over 200 Protestants burnt at the stake in a campaign to rid her kingdom of blasphemers. It is said she watched the burnings at Smithfield with dedicated fervour.

Elizabeth I: 1558–1603
The Virgin Queen. The Faerie Queen. Good Queen Bess. Last Tudor Queen. Her reign was a magnificent one – a golden age of literature, exploration and relative

peace. Her secret? Many believe it was her dedication and devotion to her role as monarch, marrying herself to her people and not multi-tasking with husbands and children.

James I: 1603–1625

I of England and VI of Scotland, son of Mary, Queen of Scots, like his predecessor named his epoch – Jacobean. First of the Stuart dynasty. An eccentric with remarkable energy, nicknamed 'the wisest fool in Christendom', he was extraordinarily well read. Hated smoking, had a fearful obsession with black magic and witchcraft, and was much intrigued by Stonehenge and its druids. James was nicknamed the Law Giver because of the number of statutes he loaded on Parliament in order to bring his new kingdom into line. He firmly believed in the Divine Right of Kings, instilling this with force into his sons.

Charles I: 1625–1649

The only King of England to be beheaded, Charles loved the finer things in life and was an avid art collector and responsible for starting the Royal Collection proper, today the largest private art collection in the world. Imprudently refused to consult Parliament for over 10 years and eventually the land erupted into Civil War. It was the king's refusal to say die that led to his death. When offered peace by the republicans he tried to restart the war. Arrested, he stood trial for treason against his people and was executed on 30 January 1649.

Charles II: 1660–1685

Excessive, exuberant, the Merry Monarch lived up to his nickname. Keen to be popular (and keen also to keep his head), Charles opened up royal hunting grounds as public parks, established new theatres and encouraged their managements to allow women to perform in their productions. When we talk of the restoration, this is the man who started the ball rolling.

James II: 1685–1688

The last of the Stuarts. James had inherited his father's imprudence and none of his brother's tact and charm. He flaunted his Catholicism in the face of his Protestant country to such a degree that they replaced him in the Glorious Revolution with his Protestant daughter, Mary, and her husband William of Orange.

William III and Mary II: 1688–1694/1702

The only dual reigning monarchs, William was already King of Holland and insisted on having level pegging with his wife Mary when she was crowned queen. Mary – meek and mild – agreed. The couple transformed Hampton Court and